Maritime and Coastguard Agency

Code of Practice for Controlling Risks due to Noise on Ships

LONDON: TSO

information & publishing solutions

Published by TSO (The Stationery Office) and available from:

Online
www.tsoshop.co.uk

Mail, Telephone, Fax & E-mail
TSO
PO Box 29, Norwich, NR3 1GN
Telephone orders/General enquiries:
0870 600 5522
Fax orders: 0870 600 5533
E-mail: customer.services@tso.co.uk
Textphone 0870 240 3701

TSO@Blackwell and other Accredited Agents

Customers can also order publications from:
TSO Ireland
16 Arthur Street, Belfast BT1 4GD
028 9023 8451 Fax 028 9023 5401

Published for the Maritime and Coastguard Agency under licence from the
Controller of Her Majesty's Stationery Office.

The Maritime and Coastguard Agency wishes to acknowledge the expert
contribution made by the Institute of Sound and Vibration Research, based
at Southampton University in producing this code.

ISBN 978 0 11 553075 3

First published 2009

Printed in the United Kingdom for TSO
PO02325919   C15   10/09

Preface

The EC Physical Agents (Noise) Directive (2003/10/EC) is implemented for land-based workers in Great Britain by the Control of Noise at Work Regulations 2005 (SI 2005/1643) and for land-based workers in Northern Ireland by the Control of Noise at Work (Northern Ireland) Regulations 2006 (SR(NI) 2006 No.1)

For workers on ships Directive 2003/10/EC is implemented by the Merchant Shipping and Fishing Vessels (Control of Noise at Work) Regulations 2007 (SI 2007/3075).

This Code of Practice is intended to assist those concerned with designing, building, and owning or managing ships to comply with the Merchant Shipping and Fishing Vessels (Control of Noise at Work) Regulations 2007. This Code is based upon existing guidance from the Health and Safety Executive (HSE) relating to the Control of Noise at Work Regulations 2005 (herein subsequently referred to as the "2005 Noise Regulations"), but with the information edited and presented in the context of the provisions of the Merchant Shipping and Fishing Vessels (Control of Noise at Work) Regulations 2007 (herein subsequently referred to as the "2007 Noise Regulations").

Contents

1 Introduction

The Merchant Shipping and Fishing Vessel (Control of Noise at Work) Regulations 20`07 (the "2007 Noise Regulations") implement a 2003 European Council Directive on the minimum health and safety requirements regarding the exposure of workers to the risks arising from occupational noise. To implement the EU Directive for land-based workers, UK regulations have already been introduced by the Health and Safety Executive, but these land-based regulations do not apply to the master and crew of a UK ship in respect of normal shipboard activities.

The 2007 Noise Regulations extend the provisions of the EC Directive to workers in the maritime sector. No legislation, other than a general requirement to safeguard health and safety, previously existed to protect workers in the maritime sector from the risks to their heath arising from exposure to noise at work. Now, the 2007 Noise Regulations include provisions for:

action values and limit values for daily and weekly exposure to noise,

- risk assessment,
- elimination of or, where this is not reasonably practicable, reduction of exposure to noise,
- actions to be taken at action values and limit values,
- prohibition on exceeding limit values,
- provision of individual hearing protection,
- information, instruction and training for noise-exposed workers,
- health surveillance, and
- consultation with workers.

Those primarily affected by the 2007 Noise Regulations are operators and managers of ships, fishing vessels, and other marine craft, including yachts, work boats etc on which workers are employed and which are registered in the UK. The 2007 Noise Regulations apply also to charities and similar organisations that operate vessels, but only when there are paid workers on such vessels.

The main provisions of the 2007 Noise Regulations may be seen in the overview of Appendix A. Employers are required to identify which of their employees may be at risk from noise, to assess the degree of risk and to introduce measures to eliminate or minimise that risk. Enforcement of the 2007 Noise Regulations is the responsibility of the Maritime and Coastguard Agency. As the regulations are intended to improve the health and safety of workers on-board UK ships and fishing vessels, the regulations contain sanctions for non-compliance.

2 Scope of the Code

This Code of Practice deals with:

- the assessment of noise risk onboard ships,

- the measurement of noise levels,

- the determination of noise exposure levels for individual workers, or classes of workers performing the same tasks but on different watches,

- the means of protecting the seafarer from the risk of noise-induced hearing damage when it is not technically feasible or reasonably practicable to limit noise exposure to a non-harmful level, and

- noise control measures generally applicable onboard ships.

The provisions of this Code are not intended to apply to passenger spaces, except in cases where crew are required to work in such spaces. Then, such passenger spaces will be regarded as crew work areas.

Seafarers may be subject to a degree of noise not necessarily arising from their work, but at levels that might degrade speech communication or crew comfort. For such cases, Marine Guidance Note 352 contains recommendations of maximum noise levels for spaces normally used by crew members; see Appendix B.

3 Purpose of the Code

The key objective of the 2007 Noise Regulations is to limit noise levels onboard ship, and thus to protect seafarers from occupational noise which might cause noise-induced hearing loss (NIHL).

The objectives of this Code are to:

- explain the duties of employers regarding the assessment and control of hearing risk due to noise in the maritime environment,

- provide sufficient information to enable employers to assess the risks of noise injury to seafarers,

- set out measures to be taken to control that risk, either by appropriate design and use of equipment or by the use of methods to limit noise exposures on ships,

- set out the requirements to monitor the hearing health of seafarers, and

- discuss the employer's duties to inform seafarers of the risks and consequences of noise exposure, and to provide adequate training for the safe use of machinery.

It is assumed that the readers of this Code will include ship owners/managers, masters, officers, and other interested parties such as ship designers and builders. A degree of technical knowledge is assumed, but not necessarily in the field of acoustics or noise control. It is recognised that any single individual is unlikely to have the necessary range of knowledge and skills to deal effectively with all of the objectives of this Code. To fulfil all the requirements of the 2007 Noise Regulations, an employer will probably have to use a number of technical specialists, found either in-house or contracted-in.

4 Application of the Code

The 2007 Noise Regulations apply to all vessels registered in the United Kingdom on which workers are employed, whether in UK inland waters or the territorial sea or anywhere else in the world. The guidance in this Code applies to all such vessels.

This Code is also relevant to United Kingdom vessels involved in civil protection services or public service activities, and to non-UK-registered ships and vessels when they are in UK waters.

Privately-owned pleasure craft fall within the scope of this Code if there are paid crew on such craft.

The Code covers the safety of crew, regardless of nationality. It applies to crew when they are on-board for the purpose of work, whether the vessel is in port, or at sea, including time when they are off duty.

The 2007 Noise Regulations apply to noise arising from the provision of music, both live and recorded, and other entertainment activities for the benefit of paying passengers on ships. This Code applies to members of the crew exposed to the noise of such music and entertainment. Separate HSE guidance entitled *Sound Advice* contains practical guidelines on the control of noise at work arising from music and entertainment.

On sea-going ships, i.e. all ships certificated for voyages at sea, the employer's responsibilities and duties with respect to the Exposure Limit Values of the 2007 Noise Regulations do not come into force until 6 April 2011. This will allow time for compliance to be achieved. However, this extension should not be seen as justifying delaying any changes until that date if compliance can be achieved earlier. After 6 April 2011, all aspects of the 2007 Noise Regulations will be in force.

5 Effects of noise on crew

Long-term exposure to excessive noise can lead to permanent hearing damage, most commonly a loss of hearing sensitivity, that is, the ability to perceive very quiet sounds. As well as degrading the thresholds of hearing, excessive noise can also cause tinnitus; this can be a continuous and inescapable ringing or buzzing in the ears or head.

Noise-induced hearing loss (NIHL) is a leading cause for compensation claims according to the Association of British Insurers. NIHL is also a "prescribed disease" under the Industrial Injuries Disability Benefit Scheme. Under this Scheme, long-term work in ships' engine rooms is recognised as a noise-hazardous occupation.

In the marine environment, the most likely cause of occupational NIHL will be using or being near noisy machines for many hours per day, day after day, for years, possibly even a working lifetime. Over the days and years, the injury from hazardous noise will mount up imperceptibly to produce **irreversible** hearing damage. This damage is actually located within receptor "hair cells" of the inner ear, which change the vibrating motion of sound waves into electrical nerve impulses for the brain to interpret. Long-lasting noise at a very high level eventually kills these hair cells.

The human hearing system functions over a very wide range of sound frequencies: 20 Hz to 20 000 Hz. However, NIHL affects a relatively narrow range of frequencies. In the first few years of dangerous noise exposure, the damage becomes manifest as a hearing loss around 4000 Hz (4 kHz); this is the most sensitive frequency region of human hearing. As NIHL grows worse, the hearing loss becomes greater and spreads out to affect the frequencies between 3 kHz and 6 kHz. These are perceived as very high frequencies, but the range contains quite a number of the consonants of human speech.

Workers with noise-damaged hearing will notice after a few years that they don't "hear" (actually understand) conversation as well as they used to. To the noise-damaged ear, speech sounds muffled and confused, but not necessarily quieter. Trying to communicate in a competing noise becomes difficult. The NIHL then becomes a social disability. The situation becomes worse as the noise continues over the years, and natural age-associated hearing loss starts to develop. The older worker with NIHL then becomes aware of – and frustrated by – a serious social disability. However, NIHL is not limited to older workers. If there is a high noise exposure from a young age, then affected individuals may notice a significant hearing deterioration at a much younger age than normally expected.

Noise-induced hearing loss in a seafarer may compromise that worker's employment prospects. Every seafarer is required to have a Medical Fitness Certificate; hearing ability is one of the examination areas. Poor hearing requiring the use of a hearing aid may be acceptable in catering staff where sound communication is not safety critical. However, use of a hearing aid is not currently acceptable where sound communication is critical, as with watchkeeping staff. As hearing aid technology improves, this restriction will be reviewed periodically.

Noise-induced hearing loss is **preventable**. The 2007 Noise Regulations are intended to control or eliminate injurious noise in the maritime environment.

6 Assessment of noise risks

Regulation 6 of the 2007 Noise Regulations requires that the employer must assess the risk of shipboard noise to the health and safety of crew members. A suitable and sufficient "risk assessment" must be made to identify the noise risks to seafarers arising in the normal course of their work or duties, for the purpose of identifying:

- groups of workers at particular risk in the performance of their duties, and
- the measures to be taken to comply with the employer's duties under the 2007 Noise Regulations.

As part of this risk assessment, the employer should:

- identify workers who may be at risk from work noise,
- estimate or evaluate those workers' noise exposures and compare them with the exposure action values and exposure limit values in the 2007 Noise Regulations,
- identify the available risk controls,
- identify the steps planned to control and monitor risks from noise, and
- record the assessment, including the steps that have been taken and their effectiveness.

Note the phrase "estimate or evaluate" above. The assessment may well be a quick initial estimate of noise risks, followed by a series of detailed measurements to quantify the risk of noise to exposed workers.

6.1 Initial estimation of noise risk

The noise assessor will find it most efficient to conduct an initial walk-round through all compartments of the vessel, to judge where noise risks may exist. This walk-round exercise may take the form of a "risk assessment". This is a paper exercise giving careful consideration to what shipboard noises could cause harm to crew members. The assessor should get a roster of those working onboard the vessel, find out where crew members work at their jobs, and ask the section supervisors about the watch duration for workers in that section. The assessor should also ask the section supervisors about any portable hand tools, either electrically-powered or air-powered, that might be used by workers, and where such tools would be used.

The risk assessment should also consider what precautions are being taken or could be taken to control the noise risks found. Workers and others have a right to be protected from harm caused by a failure to take reasonable control measures.

As an obvious starting point for a risk assessment, potentially harmful noise is quite likely in any work compartment where:

- workers have to shout to be clearly understood by someone 2 metres away;

- workers experience temporary dullness of hearing, or ringing in their ears after leaving the work space (workers should be able to describe their experiences);

- workers are subject to the sudden release of compressed air, or loud explosive noises from equipment such as cartridge-operated tools;

- workers are exposed to high-level impact noise from hammering on metal surfaces, or using chipping tools; or

- there are diesel-powered electric generators or diesel propulsion engines running in the confined space of a ship's engine room. (Ask the workers and their supervisors about these possibilities.)

It is important to keep workers and their representatives involved and informed in the assessment of noise risk. An effective partnership with workers will help to ensure the information used for the risk assessment is based on realistic assessments of the work being carried out, and the time taken to do that work.

When thinking about the paper-exercise risk assessment for noise, these distinctions should be kept in mind:

- a **hazard** is anything that may cause harm – high noise exposure causes noise-induced hearing loss, which is a form of harm, and

- the **risk** is the chance, high or low, that somebody will develop noise-induced hearing loss.

A simple but useful risk assessment may be done in five steps (Health and Safety Executive, 2006). It doesn't need to be perfect, but it does need to be done in order to *identify* and *prioritise* risks.

Step 1: **Identify the hazards**
In this case, the hazard is excessive noise. This can cause permanent hearing damage, which is a form of "ill health".

Step 2: **Decide who might be harmed and how**
Anyone exposed to excessive noise for a long time (hours per day) is at risk of developing noise-induced hearing loss. But how serious is NIHL? If it is permanent, then noise-induced hearing loss is considered to be a *moderate* harm.

Step 3: **Evaluate the risks and decide on precautions**
If the risk assessor finds a compartment that is significantly noisier than would be expected from the sounds of everyday life, it is possible that the noise levels will exceed 80 dB(A). This is comparable to the noise level of a busy street, a typical vacuum cleaner or a crowded restaurant: it will be possible to hold a conversation, but the noise will be intrusive. Working in an environment of 80 dB(A) for eight hours will result in exposure at the Lower Exposure Action Value found in the 2007 Noise Regulations

To get a rough estimate of whether noise measurements are required to quantify the noise risk, use the simple voice-communication tests below, as recommended in the HSE Guidance (2005).

Test	Likely noise level	Noise measurements will be needed if workers get this noise for more than:
The noise is intrusive, but normal conversation is possible.	80 dB(A)	6 hours
You have to shout to talk to someone 2 metres away.	85 dB(A)	2 hours
You have to shout to talk to someone 1 metre away.	90 dB(A)	45 minutes

If a noisy workspace or work process is found to fail any of these three voice tests, then a series of measurements will be necessary for an accurate quantification of the affected workers' noise exposures.

Step 4: Record your findings and implement them

It is important that the risk assessor records which shipboard work areas seem to present a noise risk. In respect of the identified noisy areas, the recommendation will be that a full noise assessment be performed by a competent person, and a date by which the assessment survey should be completed. This is the important result. The noise assessment should include comments on noise control measures to reduce noise exposures to the lowest level "reasonably practicable".

The risk assessment should be retained by the employer.

Step 5: Review your assessment and update if necessary

The risk assessment must be reviewed periodically, at suitable intervals. A review will be necessary if:

■ there are significant changes in working conditions that affect its validity; or

■ if developing NIHL (shown by hearing health surveillance) indicates that a further risk assessment is necessary.

Each review should be recorded. If a periodic review identifies a need for any changes to procedures or practices, these changes shall be made. The records of periodic reviews should be retained.

6.2 Quantification of noise risk

When the initial risk assessment identifies harmful noise, the noise assessor will make measurements to quantify accurately the exposed workers' personal noise exposure. It is important at this stage to distinguish between noise level and noise exposure. Noise *exposure* depends both on noise *level* and on the *duration* of the noise. A high level noise for a short time will give the same noise exposure as a lower level noise for a longer time, if both noises contain the same amount of acoustic energy.

For the most part, the level of an occupational noise is measured in A-weighted decibels, dB(A). The A-weighting is a frequency weighting within the measuring instrument, to account for the response of the human ear. Like noise levels, noise exposure levels are A-weighted and expressed in dB(A) averaged over a notional eight hour work period, although the actual work period may longer **or** shorter. A worker's **d**aily **P**ersonal **E**xposure **L**evel would be reported in dB(A) $L_{EP,d}$. If a worker's $L_{EP,d}$ values are markedly different from day to day, the 2007 Noise Regulations allow the averaging of the daily values over a notional five day week. That worker's **W**eekly **P**ersonal **E**xposure **L**evel would be reported in dB(A) $L_{EP,w}$.

Potentially harmful noise may also occur with very high levels lasting only a very short time. The regulations specify that measurements of instantaneous peak sound pressure level should be considered. These peak levels are C-weighted, to account for the frequency range of human hearing (between 20 Hz and 20 kHz); peak levels are reported in dB(C) L_{Cpeak}.

The 2007 Noise Regulations give action values and limit values in terms of the $L_{EP,d}$ or $L_{EP,w}$, and the L_{Cpeak} for each exposed worker.

The lower exposure action values are:

- a daily or weekly personal noise exposure of 80 dB(A); and

- a peak sound pressure level of 135 dB(C).

The upper exposure action values are :

- a daily or weekly personal noise exposure of 85 dB(A); and

- a peak sound pressure level of 137 dB(C).

In applying the lower and upper exposure action values, no account shall be taken of the attenuation provided by personal hearing protectors provided by the employer for the use of his workers.

The exposure limit values are:

- a daily or weekly personal noise exposure of 87 dB(A); and

- a peak sound pressure level of 140 dB(C).

In applying the exposure limit values, account shall be taken of any attenuation provided by individual hearing protectors provided by the employer for the use of his workers.

If any of these exposure action and limit values are exceeded, duties may fall upon the employer and upon the employees; these duties will be discussed in later sections. In addition to any specific duties, there is a general duty upon employers. Employers must ensure that the risk from the exposure of employees to noise is either eliminated at source or, where this is not reasonably practicable, reduced to as low a level as is reasonably practicable. This phrase "reasonably practicable" does not mean simply achievable; it involves a reasoned and efficient balance between *risk* and *remedy*. The employer should be prepared to justify the reasonable practicability of any remedy implemented or rejected.

6.3 Preparing for the survey

If the risk assessment recommended a noise assessment, this will be to quantify the noise exposure of workers performing tasks that present a hazard to hearing. Exposure is a combination of noise level and noise duration for any task or shift; noise level is something that can be measured, while duration can be measured or reported by the worker.

6.3.1 General considerations – Choice of instrument

In order to determine the amount of noise energy to which employees are being exposed, it is necessary to carry out a noise survey. Noise measurement instruments are designed to respond in approximately the same way as the human ear, and to give objective reproducible measurements of sound level. Given that an increase of only 3 dB(A) will halve the permitted period of exposure, it is important that noise measurements are accurate.

Measurement of sound levels should be carried out using a hand-portable meter suitable for field use; the instrument should be manufactured to satisfy the requirements of BS EN 61672-1:2003. This Standard specifies two classes of instrument, based upon performance tolerances. A class 1 sound level meter may be thought of as a precision-grade instrument; a class 2 is an industrial- or survey-grade meter. The main difference between the grades is in the tolerance band allowed for microphone directivity, and for frequency-weighting filter networks.

The survey instrument must have an averaging function, to calculate automatically the equivalent continuous sound level over the sample time of any measurement made. Modern sound level meters are very powerful, to the extent that they can report several different noise measurements, all made simultaneously during a single noise sample period. The sound level meter (SLM) must be able to report equivalent continuous sound levels (L_{eq} values) measured using the A-weighting (to mimic the frequency response of the human ear) and the C-weighting (essentially a flat frequency response over the frequency range of human hearing, 20 Hz to 20 kHz); these measurements would be L_{Aeq} and L_{Ceq}, respectively. The A and C frequency weightings may be seen in Figure 1 found on the next page. The recorded L_{Aeq} values will be used to calculate $L_{EP,d}$ values of noise-exposed workers, for comparison with the action values of the 2007 Noise Regulations.

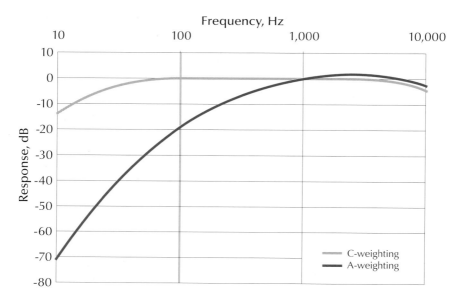

Figure 1 The frequency responses of the A-weighting (green line) and the C-weighting (grey line). The horizontal scale is frequency in hertz (Hz). The vertical scale is the response in decibels (dB) relative to 1000 Hz. Note that the A-weighting discriminates against very low frequencies of sound; the negative sign indicates an attenuation of the low-frequency energy of the sound being measured.

Together, the L_{Aeq} and L_{Ceq} values will be useful in assessing low-frequency noise, and in picking suitable hearing protectors for an occupational noise environment.

The measurement instrument must also be able to measure and report the instantaneous peak sound pressure levels L_{Cpk} of impulse/impact noises to which workers might be exposed. Such noises may be defined as a noise event of short duration which occurs as an isolated event or as one of a series of events with a repetition rate of less than 15 per second. (An example of impulse noise aboard a ship is the starting air release on some slow-speed engines; an impact noise might be the blow of a hammer.) Meters will usually report the highest L_{Cpk} occurring at any time during the noise sampling period. This value should be compared to the action and limit values of the 2007 Noise Regulations. Ensure that the sound level meter is capable of measuring instantaneous peak sound pressure levels up to 140 dB L_{Cpk}, the exposure limit value.

The instrument may also have an integrating function to measure *Sound Exposure Level*. This measurement can be very useful in quantifying impact/impulse noise, either one acoustic event, or many events occurring in a train or sequence. Sound exposure level takes all the acoustic energy of a noise sample, and presents that energy as if it lasted for a notional one second duration. The unit is dB(A) SEL.

Where a seafarer moves from task to task over a watch, or is working in tight spaces where access for noise measurements is difficult, a personal sound exposure meter (dosemeter) is an alternative means of measuring that worker's noise exposure. The instrument microphone is typically positioned on the collar or shoulder, to measure the sound near the head.

Dosemeters measure of the total sound energy received during the sampling period; this dose is given in units of Pascal squared hours ($Pa^2.h$) or as a percentage of the Upper Exposure Action Value 85 dB(A) $L_{EP,d}$. Some instruments (logging dosemeters) have the capability to record how the sound level varies throughout the sampling period: it might be informative to know the times when high and low levels occur during the sample.

There are several caveats regarding the use of a wearable dosemeter, in preference to an SLM:

■ Ensure that the dosemeter is set to an exchange rate (trading relationship) of 3 dB for doubling or halving of noise duration; this is a straight energy trade-off. Other trading relationships may be available in the instrument (for instance 5 dB), to comply with standards of other nations.

■ The noise assessor should be aware that a personal dosemeter samples all the acoustic energy over the measurement duration. The instrument is not designed to read-out L_{Cpk} values, which figure in the exposure action values.

■ A worker wearing a dosemeter should be instructed not to interfere with the instrument or microphone during the course of the measurements. The worker should also be cautioned against unnecessary speech; the wearer's voice will be included in the total acoustic energy sampled over the measurement duration.

6.3.2 Octave band analysis capability

The SLM will be more useful if it is able to give detailed data on the frequency content of each noise being surveyed. It should be able to analyse any noise sample to give octave band levels, determined simultaneously with the L_{Aeq}, L_{Ceq} and highest L_{Cpk}.

The analysis feature of the meter should cover a range of octave bands. As a minimum specification, the "lowest" octave band should be centred at 63 Hz, with the "highest" band centred at 8000 Hz. This range of octave band levels will allow calculation of the noise reduction offered by any type of hearing protector, to judge if a particular protector is adequate for the noise(s) sampled. Of course, such a calculation requires the hearing protector attenuation data (from the manufacturer).

6.3.3   Calibrator

The manufacturer of the sound level meter will have supplied a calibrator with the instrument; this device should be manufactured to satisfy the requirements of BS EN 60942:2003. The calibrator is an electroacoustic device producing a signal of known frequency (usually 1 kHz) at a known sound pressure level (94 dB is preferred as it represents an acoustic pressure of 1 pascal (Pa), but other levels such as 84 dB, 104 dB or 114 dB may be produced). The calibrator is used in the field to lock the known calibration level into the meter at the beginning of a measurement series, and to check for drift of the meter reading at the end of a measurement series.

Calibrators for use with class 1 (precision grade) sound level meters should be accurate to within ± 0.4 dB, and accurate to within ± 0.75 dB for use with class 2 (industrial grade) meters.

6.3.4   Periodic testing of instruments

At intervals not exceeding two years, the sound measuring instrument and its calibrator should be returned to the manufacturer or other competent organisation capable of providing a calibration check traceable to the UK National Physical Laboratory. If either the sound level meter or the calibrator develops a fault that affects its performance, and is repaired, it should be recalibrated following the repair. Such periodic and post-repair checks ensure that the meter and calibrator continue to comply with the appropriate British and international standards. Retain all calibration certificates for as long as the instruments remain in use.

6.3.5   Microphone wind screen

A microphone windscreen should be used during all measurements. The windscreen should not appreciably affect the calibration of the sound level meter; in general, the plastic foam types provided by the major instrument suppliers are suitable.

There are two reasons to use a windscreen during all measurements. First, and most obvious, where there is wind or air movement, turbulence of the air over the microphone would be interpreted as low-frequency sound, giving a falsely-high reading of sound level. Use a windscreen when taking readings on bridge wings or on deck. Below decks, there may be substantial air movement. Measurements of noise from ventilation inlet and output openings should be taken at positions located at 30° to the direction of flow, at a distance of 1 metre from the edge of the opening to avoid low-frequency turbulence in the air stream. Similar care should be taken near engine air intake and exhaust outlets.

Windscreens do not completely prevent interference by wind. To make reliable measurements, the apparent sound level caused by the wind should be at least 10 dB below the sound level of the source that must be measured. The manufacturer of the windscreen and meter should provide advice on the apparent noise levels generated by wind of various velocities blowing over the windscreen. For instance, the supplier might state that wind speeds of 25 to 30 km/hour (about 13 to 16 knots) blowing over the windscreen produce an apparent noise level of about 45 dB(A), so measurements of 55 dB(A) or greater could be made in this situation. If possible, measure the apparent sound level of the wind alone, then the ship noise of interest plus the wind. If the ship noise (in wind) is at least 10 dB(A) more than the wind noise only, then the ship noise reading should be accurate.

The second reason for always using a windscreen is not so obvious: protecting the microphone. The survey SLM is an expensive electroacoustic instrument; the most expensive single component is the microphone. The windscreen will cushion the microphone against minor knocks (and possible repair and re-calibration fees). The windscreen may also be regarded as a safety feature benefiting any worker subject to noise readings. The noise assessor will be sampling the noise level close to the worker's head; the assessor will wish to avoid injuring that worker who might make a sudden and unexpected movement and collide with the instrument.

6.3.6   Safety when using measuring equipment

The survey SLM and calibrator may present an ignition hazard if used in areas where flammable gas/air mixtures are present onboard ship. If noise measurements are required where fuel or cargo gases may present a hazard, then the instrument used should be certified "intrinsically safe" by BASEEFA. Consult the instrument supplier to be sure that the instruments are not potential ignition sources.

6.4 Evaluation and assessment of exposures

The aim of the noise assessment is to:

- identify the workers at risk from hearing damage (so an action plan to control noise exposure can be prepared);

- determine the daily/weekly personal noise exposure of workers, in dB(A) $L_{EP,d}$ or dB(A) $L_{EP,w}$; and

- identify additional considerations necessary for complying with the 2007 Noise Regulations, eg whether noise control measures or hearing protection are needed, and, if so, where and what type.

6.4.1 Competent persons

An onboard noise assessment should be performed by a "competent person". This person may be an employee of the ship owner/operator, or an external consultant contracted to the ship owner/operator or employer.

It is not necessary for the assessor to have an academic qualification in acoustics to enable him/her to be considered a competent person. The important factors are that the assessor has sufficient training or knowledge including practical experience using sound-measuring equipment, and other relevant qualities to undertake on-board noise assessments. These qualities will include an adequate general knowledge of vessel structure and layout, and an awareness of the work schedules and practices used onboard the vessel being surveyed. Lastly, the competent noise assessor should be aware of his or her own limitations, and take care to remain within his or her knowledge and experience.

6.4.2 Before the survey

Before starting any detailed survey, the noise assessor should have available a plan of the ship, showing all decks and compartments where hazardous noise may be found. Such plans will be used in matching noise readings to individual sources.

6.4.2.1 Operating conditions at sea

Measurements should be taken with the ship loaded or in ballast, or at some intermediate condition by agreement with the shipowner. Alternatively, if a subjective or substantial increase in noise is noticed or expected under another condition, measurements should be taken under this condition.

The main propulsion machinery should be run at normal service speed. Air conditioning, ventilation plant and auxiliary machinery (such as diesel generators) should be operated at full capacity. If these conditions cannot be achieved, or special conditions prevail, an explanation should be provided in the survey report.

Spaces containing emergency diesel engines driving generators, fire pumps or other emergency equipment that would normally be run only in an emergency, or for drill purposes, should be measured with the equipment operating.

Ships fitted with bow thrusters, stabilizers, etc may be subject to high noise levels when these are operating. Measurements should be taken at workers' positions around such machinery, and in adjacent work spaces when such machinery is operating.

6.4.2.2 Operating conditions in port

Measurements of workers' noise exposure should be taken with the ship in the "in port" condition.

Holds and deck areas, some machinery spaces may show high noise levels when the ship is loading or discharging cargo. When this is the case, measurements in such spaces should be taken with the ship's own cargo handling equipment in operation. Noise originating from sources external to the ship, such as the use of shore-based cranes etc, may need to be included where such noise represents an everyday contribution to workers' occupational noise when in port.

When the ship is a vehicle carrier and noise comes from the vehicles during loading and discharging, the noise level for workers on the vehicle decks should be measured as the cargo vehicles are being moved.

It will be necessary to take measurements at workers' positions in machinery spaces with the auxiliary machinery operating in the "in port" condition during maintenance, overhaul or similar periods alongside.

6.4.2.3 Environmental conditions

The depth of water under the ship's keel and the presence of large reflecting surfaces in the ship's vicinity may affect the readings obtained at workers' positions onboard. Such conditions should be noted in the survey record.

The meteorological conditions such as wind and rain, as well as sea state, should be such that they do not influence the measurements. Wind force 4 and sea state 3 should not be exceeded. If this cannot be achieved, the actual conditions should be reported.

When carrying out measurements of noise levels on-board, care should be taken to see that noise from external sound sources, such as construction and repair work, does not influence the noise level onboard the ship at workers' locations. However, it should be borne in mind that such external noise may affect the noise exposure of seafarers working on deck in proximity to such external sources of noise.

6.4.3   Determining noise exposure duration

The noise assessor should be aware of the total number of crew and where each person works. Ask the supervisor in each section about how long (each day) each worker is exposed to potentially harmful noise. Ask also about work schedules. Noisy work may rotate on cyclical basis; assessment of weekly noise exposure may be appropriate for some crew members. Confirm all this information with individual crew members.

Record all of this information. The assessor will have to match workers with the recorded noise levels and noise durations in order to quantify individual noise exposures.

6.4.4   Determining noise levels

6.4.4.1   *Calibration*

Before starting a measurement series, ensure that the sound level meter (SLM) batteries have sufficient charge to allow for a worthwhile period of measurement. Record the fact that the batteries were found to be satisfactory. The assessor should carry a set of spare batteries during the survey. Now perform a calibration check on the meter; ensure that the SLM reading matches the target value, that is, the known sound pressure level of the calibrator. Record the calibration tone level.

Now proceed with the survey. However, if the meter's "battery low" indicator comes on during the measurement series, pause the measurements immediately, record the noise data, and apply the calibrator signal. Record the calibration tone level. Now turn the SLM off and replace the batteries; the data should be safe in the meter's memory. Restart the SLM, perform another calibration check, and record the calibration tone level. This tedious procedure will document that the meter's calibration did not drift due to battery failure.

Now finish the planned measurement series and record the data. Apply the calibrator for a post-test check. Record the calibration tone level. This will demonstrate that the calibration level did not drift or decay over the entire measurement period. Turn the instrument off.

6.4.4.2 Measurement procedure

The previous section dealt with the beginning and end of a measurement series; this section considers the actual data acquisition. Remember that the overriding aim is to characterise the noise levels for individual workers or classes of workers during their watches. The assessor should have available a roster of all seafarers working at each task in each compartment or space. The assessor should also be aware of portable hand tools used by workers in each space, or on deck, and how long such tools might be used.

What readings are needed? Average (equivalent continuous) sound level readings of reasonably steady noise and fluctuating noise should be taken in dB(A) and dB(C). It is best if these two levels can be determined simultaneously, that is, during a single noise sample. If the SLM is able to give equivalent continuous octave-band levels between 31.5 and 8 000 Hz, record these observation to assess the suitability of ear protectors that may be recommended for that working compartment.

A measuring (or sample) time of at least 60 seconds should be allowed. This should be long enough to ensure that the L_{Aeq} and L_{Ceq} readings reach a stable value, not changing more than 0.2 dB. If the equivalent (average) readings have not stabilised after 60 seconds, continue the sample until they are stable. Record the L_{Aeq} and L_{Ceq} readings to the nearest 0.5 dB.

If the noise source varies regularly in level, over a few seconds or minutes, ensure that the L_{Aeq} and L_{Ceq} samples include at least three complete cycles; an **equal** number of high-noise periods and low-noise periods are needed. If the noise source varies irregularly in level over a few seconds or minutes, capture a long sample that is stable, not varying more than 0.2 dB. Record the L_{Aeq} and L_{Ceq} readings to the nearest 0.5 dB.

If the noise source is intermittent, get stable readings for a quiet period when the source is off, **and** for a period when the source is active. Record both L_{Aeq} and L_{Ceq} readings to the nearest 0.5 dB.

During noise measurements, only those persons necessary for the operation of the ship should be present in the space concerned, with the noise assessor. The spaces should generally be furnished to the normal seagoing standard. A record should be made of all operating conditions in the workplace. Which machines are running? At what load or RPM? Ventilation on or off? Doors or hatches open or closed? Remember that comparisons will be necessary in the future, to see if the noise levels have increased with time.

Unless specifically required, noise readings should not normally be taken within 1 metre of decks, bulkheads, or other major reflecting surfaces. However, if the noise-exposed worker is close to such a reflecting surface, the assessor must "follow the ear" to sample the noise actually experienced by that worker.

In general, the microphone should be located with its direction of greatest sensitivity (or direction for which it is calibrated) towards the noise source. This usually means pointing the microphone directly at the noise source, but consult the SLM instructions beforehand. In spaces that do not contain predominant noise sources, point the microphone upwards.

The assessor should bear in mind that his own body is a reflecting surface, and that his clothing is absorptive. If the SLM is held close to the body, this will cause errors in the observed sound levels, by perhaps 2 dB(A); hold the SLM out at arm's length to avoid these errors.

To get a reading for a particular worker, the SLM microphone should be held alongside the worker's head, approximately 0.2 metre from the ear. Basing the microphone location on this shoulder-ear location should take care of any consideration of standing- or sitting-ear height. If the noise is clearly coming from one side, then measure near the ear on that side. Otherwise, either ear will do.

Record whether the worker is stationary or moving. If the measurement subject moves, the microphone must move to **follow the ear**. Try to be aware of which way the measurement subject will move. There is no wish to interfere with that worker's job. Neither is there a wish to have a minor collision between the worker's head and the microphone (another reason to use the microphone windscreen ... to protect the worker and to protect the instrument).

How long should the noise sample be? This depends on the character of the noise. If the sound is reasonably steady in level, then a minute or so should give steady readings for L_{Aeq} and L_{Ceq}. If after one minute, the L_{eq} values have not reached a steady value (no more than 0.2 dB variation), then keep on measuring until the L_{eq} values are stable.

If the sound is cyclical over a long period, minutes to an hour say, then at least one COMPLETE cycle of the long-term noise fluctuation must be captured. The more COMPLETE noise cycles measured, the better representation of the true L_{Aeq}. However, if the noise cycle lasts hours, it may be better to get a short sample of the L_{Aeq} during each part of the noise cycle, then use the HSE "Ready Reckoner" to sum up for the L_{Aeq} of the whole cycle. See Appendix C for the HSE Ready Reckoner and how it may be used.

If sampling for a long cycle, an SLM tripod is useful for acquiring a lengthy sample at a worker's duty station. The assessor should **never** leave the SLM unattended during a measurement. It is not unknown for workers to sing, shout or clap for the SLM just to see the display change. Such actions may have an effect on the measurement in progress: the L_{Cpeak} could be erroneous, but the L_{Aeq} and L_{Ceq} values will probably not be affected greatly (or at all). If this does happen, at least the surveyor will be present to see it happen, and will be able to judge the necessity of discarding the data and starting another sample.

There may be occasions when there is no worker currently available to keep watch on a particular machine or engine. In this case, the assessor may position the SLM microphone about 0.2 metre from his own ear and walk around the noise source, keeping 1 metre from the base plate or frame of the source. Record the level and the fact that a walk-around was performed, due to the absence of a machine operator.

Throughout this data acquisition phase, record the observed levels for each operator or class of worker, together with a note of the measurement locations within the compartment. Such notes will guide the recommendations for the establishment of Ear Protection Zones. It is imperative that the noise assessor is able to match up the noise observations to all workers on all decks throughout the vessel. It is also important to ensure that the assessor has accounted for all seafarers who may be exposed to hazardous noise: recall the need for a crew roster mentioned before, to account for all the crew members.

During the noise survey, the assessor may find it useful to record his observations on a worksheet, such as that laid out in Table 1 on the next page. (Such worksheets will prove useful in the preparation of the Noise Assessment Report; see Appendix D.) At the top of the worksheet are spaces for important information about the survey: the name of the vessel and its location during the survey (in a named port, or on passage between named ports); date; assessor's name; etc. Enter the calibration level observed before a measurement series: this demonstrates that a calibration field-check was actually performed. At the end of a measurement series, enter the post-test calibration level on the final page of observed levels: this demonstrates that the SLM calibration was stable throughout the measurement series.

The first column is to identify individual workers, or classes of workers. Record the task, duty or job in the second column, along with some notation giving the worker-location referenced to the plan of the vessel (to accompany the survey report).

The sample duration is straightforward: how long was the measurement sample for this worker or task? Enter the L_{Aeq} observed over the sample duration. Now enter the noise exposure duration appropriate to that worker or that duty: fractions of an hour will be adequate ... for instance ¼ hour, or 4½ hours. There is no need to fill in the Exposure Points or $L_{EP,d}$ while acquiring the noise data; save this job for some quiet time.

There are only two more columns to be filled in during the survey. Enter the highest instantaneous peak L_{Cpeak} observed during the sample duration. If there are comments or remarks, enter a number in the final, right-hand column. Enter the actual numbered comment on a line at the bottom of the sheet. This completes the measurements and record for one seafarer or job; proceed to work through the crew roster.

6.4.5 Calculating Daily Personal Noise Exposure

For each individual (or job) on the worksheet of Table 1, there is an observed L_{Aeq} and a noise exposure duration. These two entries will be used with the Health and Safety Executive Ready Reckoner found in Appendix C. The method is straightforward: find the column for the appropriate noise exposure duration, then find the row for the recorded L_{Aeq}. Where the column and row intersect, find the Exposure Points for the worker. Now go to the two right-hand columns with the worker's Exposure Points; find the $L_{EP,d}$ for your worker.

A quick look at the Ready Reckoner values will explain how it works. Find the intersection between the 85 dB(A) L_{eq} and 8 hours. This is 100 Exposure Points, which is equal to 85 dB(A) $L_{EP,d}$. Think of this as 100% of a "bad noise day". Refer to Appendix C for further explanation of the workings of the Exposure Point system, and how it may be used for adding varying levels for component tasks comprising one job or one workday. There is also information on daily and weekly exposures.

Once familiar with Exposure Points, the noise assessor can easily complete the missing columns of the worksheet(s), which include a row for each noise-exposed employee or class of worker. The worksheet(s) could be added to the noise report, as an attachment or appendix. The noise readings will certainly have to be recorded.

Table 1. Worksheet: Measurement observations and results

vessel:										
date:		surveyor:					start calibration level:			
vessel location during survey:							end calibration level:			
name/job	activity/location/ tool use	position on ship plan	time of day	sample duration	meas. level, LAeq	exposure duration	Exposure Points	LEP,d	LCpeak	see remarks below

LEP,d
LAeq
LCpeak

numbered remarks (from above):

6.5 Survey Reporting and Periodic Reviews

The 2007 Noise Regulations require that the employer assess the level of noise to which workers are exposed. The noise assessment should identify individual workers (or groups of workers) who are at risk from the shipboard noise, and any measures already in place, or needed, to comply with the employer's duties under the regulations.

This noise assessment must be planned and carried out by a competent person, who then prepares a suitable and sufficient report of the assessment findings and results. As a guide, the noise assessment should identify workers by name or by task, and report the noise level(s) to which they are exposed and for how long. The assessment should pinpoint the location of the workers when they are at risk from noise. The simplest way to achieve this would be to link the L_{Aeq}, L_{Ceq} and L_{Cpeak} readings to noise measurement locations indicated on a detailed plan of the ship. Such a location plan will be useful when it comes time to review the noise assessment: the reviewer must be able to return to the area of documented noise risk.

It is important that the noise assessment specifies:

- whether the exposure action values or the exposure limit values have been exceeded, and

- the measures the employer has taken or intends to take to comply with his duties under the 2007 Noise Regulations.

The noise assessor may be working on behalf of the employer of the ship's crew; the assessor will most probably not be a noise control engineer working on behalf of the ship owner. However, the noise assessor may be in a position to influence the measures that the employer "intends to take". The noise assessment report should make general recommendations for noise abatement measures by technical means that affect the noise levels experienced by the seafarers. Reduce the noise at source. Block or interfere with the noise transmission path. Finally, if no reduction or blocking is "reasonably practicable", protect the receiver. Remember that crew training will be necessary to ensure effective use of any noise abatement measures put into effect.

Any noise abatement measures that are recommended, and any implementation timetables suggested, are for the owner, ship manager or employer to consider. The ship owner will have to decide on any noise reduction measures involving the engines or structure of the vessel. The ship manager or employer will have to seek expert advice concerning other workable noise exposure reduction methods (not calling for a re-fit), and judge if such methods are reasonably practicable.

General recommendations should also include some mention of organisational or management means, usually "people solutions" aimed at controlling or limiting workers' noise duration. Any alterations to working schedules or watch lengths will require consultation with the crew members and their representatives.

It would be prudent if a copy of the noise assessment report were carried onboard the vessel to which it applies. Whilst the 2007 Noise Regulations do not specify the format for any noise survey report, a report in the form set out in Appendix D might be carried onboard the vessel to which it applies. Regardless of the format, the completed noise assessment must be retained by the employer, although the 2007 Noise Regulations give no indication for low long. As an absolute minimum, a noise assessment report should be retained until the follow-on (repeat) noise survey report has been received. A prudent, long-term view would be to retain any noise assessment report for 40 years, until all employees whose noise exposures are recorded in the report have retired from work.

The 2007 Noise Regulations also require that noise assessment reports are reviewed:

- at "suitable" intervals;

- if there are any significant changes in working condition which affect the validity of the risk assessment or noise assessment, e.g. when a ship has been re-engined, when changes in a ships' structural arrangement have been made which are likely to affect noise; or

- if the results of health surveillance (monitoring audiometry) reveal some crew members with developing noise-induced hearing damage, thus indicating that the noise control and hearing conservation measures have failed.

Review of an assessment does not necessarily mean a repeat of an assessment. A review should be a consideration of whether the original assessment is still valid. Any such review should be recorded. If the review finds that noise conditions onboard the vessel have changed (as might be expected after an engine re-fit), *then* a repeat noise assessment will be necessary.

7 Avoiding or reducing exposure to noise

The following hierarchy should be adopted for establishing priorities in a programme of measures to safeguard the safety and health of seafarers:

i.   avoiding risks;

ii.   evaluating the risks which cannot be avoided;

iii.   combating the risks at source;

iv.   adapting the work to the individual, especially as regards the design of work places, the choice of work equipment and the choice of working and production methods;

v.   adapting to technical progress;

vi.   replacing the noisy by the non-noisy or the less noisy ;

vii.   developing a coherent overall prevention policy which covers technology, organization of work, working conditions, social relationships and the influence of factors related to the working environment;

viii.   giving collective protective measures priority over individual protective measures; and

ix.   giving appropriate instructions to the workers.

7.1   Developing a control strategy

The risk assessment should enable methods for controlling exposure to be identified. When considering the noise exposures, the assessor should be thinking about the work processes that cause them. Understanding why workers are exposed to noise will aid identification of methods for reducing or eliminating the risk.

The important stages in this management process are:

- identifying the chief sources of noise for an individual or a class of workers who are all exposed to the same sources;

- ranking the sources in terms of their contribution to the total risk;

- identifying and evaluating potential noise solutions that are useful and cost effective;

- establishing targets which can be realistically achieved;

- allocating priorities and establishing an 'action programme';

- defining management responsibilities and allocating adequate resources;

- implementing the action programme;

- monitoring progress; and

- evaluating the success of the programme.

The approach taken to reducing noise risks will depend on the practical aspects of individual jobs, tasks or processes found in place, and on the current levels of exposure. Look at the problem to separate source, path and receiver. Engineering a fix will attack the noise level; managing a "people solution" can work on the noise duration.

The employer may also need to adapt the noise controls for workers who are at particular risk of injury, for instance, those workers who are more susceptible to noise injury and have shown developing hearing loss at exposures below the exposure action values. The 2007 Noise Regulations also call for the employer to "consider" so far as practicable, the effects on health and safety of workers resulting from the interaction between noise and the use of ototoxic substances (poisonous to the ears), and between noise and vibration. In addition, the employer must consider what health and safety effects might result from interactions between occupational noise and audible warning signals. Such interactions could be extreme: the work noise is at such a high level that it makes the warning inaudible; or alternatively, the warning sound is at such a high level that it poses a noise risk itself.

7.2   Involvement of workers

The successful management of noise risks relies on the involvement and support of workers, and in particular their representatives. These representatives can provide an effective channel of communication with the workers, and assist them in understanding and using health and safety information.

While some noise control solutions may be quite straightforward, others will require changes to the way in which work is organised. Such changes can only be effectively implemented in consultation with workplace representatives.

Effective consultation relies on:

- sharing with workers the relevant information about health and safety measures;

- workers being given the opportunity to express their views and complaints, and to contribute in a timely fashion to the resolution of health and safety issues; and

- the views of workers being valued and taken into account, and their complaints given reasonable consideration.

Consultation can result in better control solutions being identified that are well understood by the workers. The employer will be relying on workers to make the control measures effective, for the benefit of both the employer and the employees. Subject to adequate training and supervision, workers have a duty to make correct use of machinery and equipment, and to cooperate with the employer to ensure that the environment and working conditions are safe, with noise risks minimised and where possible eliminated. The process of consultation encourages worker involvement and co-operation with control measures and so ensures that controls are more likely to be successfully implemented.

7.3   Risk controls

If noise risks are identified, then Regulation 7 of the 2007 Noise Regulations requires that the employer must ensure that such noise risks are either **eliminated** at source, or **reduced** to a level that is as low as reasonably practicable. Be aware that 'reasonably practicable' implies a workable balance between risk and remedy; it does not mean simply that something is achievable (with no concern about trouble and cost).

The noise assessment may show that the upper exposure action value has been exceeded for certain employees. Then the employer must establish and implement a programme of appropriate measures, technical and/or organisational, to reduce the noise exposure of those workers. A technical measure implies something to do with plant or hardware; an organisational measure will quite likely be a "people solution" of some sort. No single technique will be appropriate for every situation.

The exposure limit values are absolute limits. Employees must not work where noise is at so high a level that the noise exposure exceeds the limit, for protected ears or unprotected ears. If exposures exceed either of the limit values, then the employer must:

- take immediate action to reduce the exposure to below the exposure limit values;

- identify the reasons why this overexposure has occurred; and

- amend the protection and prevention measures in order to avoid any recurrence.

7.3.1   Personal hearing protection

Hearing protection may be thought of as an easy solution, but this is not so. Protection should be used for two distinct, even opposing, purposes.

- When a risk assessment or noise assessment identifies workers who are exposed to potentially harmful noise, then those workers should be provided with, and use, hearing protection as "first aid" while some solution (more effective or more permanent) is put into effect.

- When no reasonably practicable technical or organisational noise solution is available, then permanent provision of hearing protection is a "last resort". Remember that 'reasonably practicable' means a workable balance between risk and remedy.

Regulation 8 of the 2007 Noise Regulations requires the employer to make hearing protection available to any worker whose noise exposure exceeds the lower exposure value; when the upper exposure action value is reached or exceeded, the employer must provide protection and ensure that his workers use the hearing protection.

7.3.1.1   Types of hearing protectors

7.3.1.1.1   Ear plugs

The simplest form of hearing protection is the ear plug, which works by fitting into the external ear canal to block noise from reaching the eardrum. Modern ear plugs are made of soft plastic in a variety of shapes and colours.

Some disposable plugs are made of easily malleable plastic foam, formed into a cylinder or cone. These are to be compressed by rolling between the fingers to make a smaller diameter, inserted into the ear canal, and held in place until they expand to conform to the shape of the canal. When the expansion is complete after a few seconds, the foam plugs make a good noise-tight seal against the skin.

There are drawbacks to such malleable plastic ear plugs. Because the plugs must be fingered during installation, they can become fouled by dirty hands. Foam plugs can be washed between insertions, for re-use a few times. Alternatively, the plugs be discarded after one use; this will become expensive after a while. The employer must ensure that sufficient supplies of disposable plugs are onboard, to last for a voyage.

Other sorts of ear plugs come pre-moulded in flexible plastic, sometimes sized for small and large ear canals. These can take fanciful shapes, resembling a mushroom or a Christmas tree. Such pre-formed plugs may be washed and re-used repeatedly.

It is also possible to acquire individually-moulded inserts for each employee. These inserts are moulded to fit the right and left ear canals of each worker; they cannot be used by anyone else. The taking of ear impressions and the associated lab work to produce the final protectors make this option **very** expensive.

Whatever type of ear plug is chosen, they will usually come in some bright colour that contrasts with the skin. This is an attempt to make them visible at a distance, so their use may be monitored.

7.3.1.1.2   Ear muffs

In general, ear muffs provide a more effective form of hearing protection. They consist of a pair of rigid plastic cups designed to completely envelope the ears; each cup is fitted with soft-sealing cushions to fit closely against the head around the ears. The ear cups are connected by a springy headband (or neck band) which ensures that the cushions press gently around each ear to produce a noise-tight seal. Different types are available and provision should be made according to the circumstances of use, possibly with other items of

Personal Protective Equipment. For instance, hearing protection may be required with hard hats. Some ear muffs have a springy band that can be rotated to become a back-of-the-neck band. Alternatively, plastic earcups with cushions may be fitted to the hard hat.

Like earplugs, muffs will usually come in some bright colour, to make them visible at a distance for easy monitoring.

7.3.1.2   Selection of appropriate protectors

When selecting Personal Hearing Protection (PHP) for issue to noise-exposed workers, the employer should give consideration to:

- types of protector, and suitability for the work being done;

- noise reduction (attenuation) offered by the protector;

- compatibility with other safety equipment;

- pattern of the noise exposure;

- the need to communicate and hear warning sounds;

- environmental factors such as heat, humidity, dust and dirt; and

- cost of maintenance or replacement.

As might be expected, there are good and not-so-good points associated with earplugs and ear muffs, as seen below.

type	advantages	disadvantages
ear plugs	• small and easily carried	• easily lost
	• cheap (at first)	• costs mount if discarded frequently
	• good protection if inserted properly	• can be difficult to insert and remove, difficult to supervise
	• comfortable in hot, humid workspaces	• hygiene problems in dirty workplace, may irritate the ear canal
	• compatible with safety headgear	
	• can be used with muffs for double protection	
	• convenient for working in confined spaces	

type	advantages	disadvantages
ear muffs	• good protection easy to supervise (easy to see) • easily fitted, popular with users, one size fits all	• protection decreases with age, seals should be replaced • more expensive, breakable • uncomfortable in hot workplaces • may clash with other safety headgear • may be inconvenient in confined spaces

See Appendix E for a discussion of how to estimate or calculate the attenuation provided by Personal Hearing Protection.

7.3.1.3   Time-of-usage is important

If Personal Hearing Protection is given to workers exposed to noise risk, then it should be worn. It should be worn for the entire duration of the noise exposure. The protection, be it muffs or plugs, gives little attenuation if it isn't applied properly to the ears.

[handwritten note: • easy to Supervise]

A worker might think that he will get half the protection if he wears the protectors for half of the noisy time. But noise exposure doesn't behave in a linear fashion like time. Half of the noisy time will have an L_{Aeq} only 3 dB down from the level for the whole of the noisy time.

Figure 2 on the next page illustrates how the effective protection of any Personal Hearing Protector is degraded when not used over the entire duration of a dangerous noise. The horizontal axis is percentage of noisy time **not** protected against a high-level noise. The vertical scale is effective attenuation or protection. There are three lines on the figure, representing a 30 dB protector (the triangle symbol), one of 20 dB (the square symbol) and another of 10 dB (the circle symbol).

Note that the effective exposure reduction of the 30 dB protector is seriously compromised after a very few minutes of non-usage. If the exposed worker has only 15 minutes of high-level noise, but wears the 30 dB protectors for the remainder of an eight-hour watch, the 30 dB protector provides only 15 dB of actual benefit. The 20 dB protector is also compromised. From the employer's viewpoint, all the benefit of paying good money for good hearing protection is lost if those protectors aren't worn, for even a few minutes of the noise day.

Workers provided with PHP will need information and training to help them use their protectors fully and properly, to gain maximum benefit.

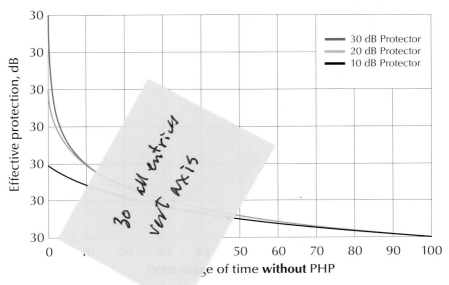

Figure 2 The effective attenuation provided by Personal Hearing Protection is reduced if it is not used all the time during noise exposure. The graph shows how time of usage affects the useful attenuation of a 30 dB protector (green), a 20 dB protector (grey) and a 10 dB protector (black). Any PHP worn for only half the exposure time will provide only about 3 dB of noise exposure reduction.

7.3.1.4 Hearing Protection Zones

Regulation 8 of the 2007 Noise Regulations calls for Hearing Protection Zones to be marked out where any worker is likely to be exposed to noise at or above the upper exposure action values 85 dB(A) $L_{EP,d}$ or 137 dB(C) L_{Cpeak}. Access to such noise-hazardous areas of the vessel should be restricted to those workers using Personal Hearing Protection. Any Hearing Protection Zone should be marked with a standardised safety sign, as seen in Figure 3 below; blue circular signs indicate a mandatory course of action, as in this case "Use hearing protection". This safety sign may also be found in Marine Guidance Note 352, Annex 2 "Use of Safety Signs".

Figure 3 The safety sign indicating mandatory use of Personal Hearing Protection. The background is blue inside a white border; the "hearing protector man" is a white outline, in contrast to the blue background.

In some cases, the mandatory blue sign may not tell the full story. A supplementary sign may be used in conjunction with the safety sign, to provide extra information. The supplementary sign must be square or rectangular, with a blue background inside a white border. The text must be in English in a white font; an additional language may be used to inform any crew members who have a limited understanding of English. The supplementary text might give a specific additional instruction, such as "Use hearing protection inside this compartment" or "Do not enter this compartment unless wearing hearing protection". The text might also provide useful safety information about the noise hazard, such as "Use hearing protection when operating this machine."

In the case of noisy hand tools, either electrically- or air-powered, the hearing protection zone moves with the tool. A small blue "hearing protection man" may be attached to the tool, the power lead or the compressed-air line. The meaning is clear: If you are going to use this tool, wear hearing protection.

The noise assessor should not recommend that the "hearing protection man" be posted without good reason. The sign is a serious instruction applicable to a serious hazard. If the safety sign is posted, then the workers are required to take note and use the protectors issued for their benefit. If the safety sign is posted, then the employer has a duty to enforce the full and proper use of hearing protectors, with disciplinary sanctions for non-compliant seafarers.

Signage quickly becomes part of the "wallpaper" of the workplace environment, especially if there are many similar blue safety signs indicating a mandatory course of action for a number of hazards. Signage by itself is not a solution to a hazard.

7.3.2   Technical or engineering noise solutions

It may be possible to find alternative work methods that eliminate or reduce exposure to noise: "Screws, not nails." This may involve substitution of alternative work processes or a quieter tool. In the extreme, thought should be given to the question: Is it necessary to manufacture or make the "product" onboard, or could it be bought in periodically during the voyage?

If it is not feasible to *eliminate* the noise at source, what about *reducing* the noise at source?

■ Consider installing anti-vibration mounts or flexible couplings to isolate vibrating machinery or components from decks and bulkheads (that act as sounding boards, radiating sound into the air). Keeping the vibration energy out of the ship structure will prevent structure-borne noise travelling around the vessel.

■ Vibrating panels on machines can also act as sounding boards. Make the panels less prone to vibrate by using damping materials to change the mass and stiffness of such panels.

■ Heating, ventilation and air-conditioning noise is a combination of aerodynamic noise (fan- and flow-generated) and mechanical noise. Consider reducing the airspeed, to reduce the aerodynamic noise.

■ High-pressure air generates turbulence-noise when vented to the atmosphere. Reduce the pressure or fit silencers.

Block or interfere with the noise transmission path between source and receiver.

■ If possible, increase the distance between source and receiver. On deck, doubling the distance can give a reduction as great as 6 dB. This reduction cannot be achieved in enclosed workspaces; the sound is echoing around within the volume.

■ Segregate noisy machinery and processes from employees in quieter areas.

■ Use barriers and screens to block the direct (loudest) path of sound to the receiver. Screens work most effectively if close to the source, or close to the receiver.

■ Consider erecting enclosures around machines. The enclosure must have a minimum of openings or leaks: the object is to trap the noise energy within the enclosure. Consider the mirror-image of the machine enclosure – a noise refuge for the potential receivers. However, this can be tricky: there must be safe access, light, ventilation, and communication to other parts of the ship.

Remember that the noise assessor may make recommendations: somebody else will have to design the noise solutions for maximum efficiency.

7.3.3   Equipment selection/purchasing/maintenance

7.3.3.1   Equipment selection

The employer should ensure that equipment selected or allocated for tasks is suitable and can do the work efficiently. Equipment that is unsuitable, or of insufficient capacity, is likely to take much longer to complete the task, and expose workers to noise for longer than is necessary.

Careful selection of consumables (e.g. abrasives for grinders and sanders) or tool accessories (such as drill bits, chisels and saw blades) can affect noise exposure. Some manufacturers supply accessories designed to reduce the noise produced. To keep up-to-date on the tools, consumables and accessories available, the employer or work supervisor should check regularly with equipment suppliers, relevant trade associations, other industry contacts and trade journals.

7.3.3.2   Purchasing policy

The employer should have (or institute) a policy on purchasing suitable equipment, taking into account both noise emission, and the requirements of the intended task. Power tool manufacturers (and importers, suppliers and tool-hire firms) should be able to help the employer select the safest and most suitable tools for defined needs.

Any organisation supplying power tools in the UK market is required to mark supplied items with the A-weighted sound power level emitted if, at the workstation, the sound pressure level exceeds 85 dB. Given a range of suitable tools or appliances, the employer should consider purchasing the specific item with the lowest A-weighted sound power level. This low-noise item may be more expensive, but the purchaser will be buying a noise solution, not a noise problem.

Manufacturers or suppliers may be willing to loan sample tools for trial. The employer should use this opportunity, and take account of workers' opinions based on practical trials. The efficiency of the tool is important: a tool that takes a long time to do the job will not be popular, and could result in a higher noise exposure (remember – noise level and noise duration) than a more efficient tool with a higher noise output.

7.3.3.3   Maintenance

Regular servicing of power tools and other work equipment will often help keep noise levels (and durations) to the minimum necessary, so:

- keep cutting tools sharp;

- lubricate any moving parts according to the manufacturer's recommendations;

- replace worn parts such as bearings and gears;

- carry out necessary balance checks and corrections; and

- replace anti-vibration mounts before they deteriorate.

The noise assessor would do well to point out to the employer that regular maintenance is always "reasonably practicable".

7.3.4   Work schedules

To control the hearing risk from noise, the assessor may recommend limiting the time workers are exposed to noise from tools, machines or processes. Every halving of the time spent in a noisy area will reduce noise exposure by 3 dB(A). This is a drastic and not particularly effective measure to limit noise exposure. However, it may be possible for workers to split their "noise day" between necessary noisy work and tasks with lower noise levels. In any case, alteration of employees' work patterns will require consultation with workers and their supervisors. Recommend that that new work patterns are adequately supervised, to ensure that workers do not drift back to the older work patterns.

7.3.5   Training and information to workers

An obvious recommendation for the noise assessor to make regards training. It is important that the employer provides operators and supervisors with information on:

- the potential injury arising from the noise of work equipment;

- the exposure limit values and the exposure action values;

- the results of the noise risk assessment and any noise measurements;
- the control measures being used to eliminate or reduce risks from noise;
- safe working practices to minimise exposure to noise;
- why and how to detect and report signs of hearing injury;
- why and how to report machines in need of maintenance;
- the circumstances in which workers are entitled to health surveillance.

The employer will be relying on the operators of noisy tools and processes to ensure the effectiveness of any control measures. The employer has a duty to consult with the workers and their representatives when implementing control measures. Workers have a duty to cooperate in the implementation of health and safety measures.

Workers should be trained in the best working techniques, including signs indicating when a machine is in need of maintenance. The manufacturer should be able to advise of any training requirements, and may offer training for operators.

Training and supervision will be required to ensure that workers are protecting themselves against potential hearing injury. Indeed, they should be encouraged to recognise and report any symptoms associated with developing hearing damage.

8 Health Surveillance

Health surveillance is about putting in place systematic, regular and appropriate procedures for the detection of work-related ill health. In the case of noise, the ill-health will be noise-induced hearing loss or tinnitus; the appropriate procedures will be regular monitoring audiometry for each individual, and acting appropriately on the findings of such hearing tests.

The primary aim of regular hearing tests is to safeguard the hearing health of seafarers. This includes identifying individuals who seem especially susceptible to noise injury, and offering these seafarers increased protection against noise, before the hearing damage becomes significant. For those individuals with an existing hearing loss, regular monitoring audiometry can verify (or otherwise) that any hearing deficit increase is consistent with natural ageing.

There is another use for regular monitoring audiometry: to check the long-term effectiveness of control measures. If workers in a certain compartment, or doing similar tasks, show developing noise-induced hearing damage, then the applicable risk assessment is inadequate, or the recommended control measures have not been effective (or indeed not implemented). A review of that "faulty" risk assessment is necessary for the appropriate workspace or work-task.

8.1 When is health surveillance required?

Regulation 10 of the 2007 Noise Regulations requires that the employer arrange or provide regular health surveillance for his noise-exposed workers. There are two levels of surveillance.

■ Where a worker is exposed to noise above the lower exposure action value(s), or where the risk assessment indicates a risk to hearing, that worker may have audiometric testing as an early warning measure.

■ If a worker is exposed to noise above the upper exposure action value(s), that worker may have his hearing examined by a doctor or by a suitably qualified person under the supervision of a doctor. The doctor should judge whether any identified hearing deficit is the likely result of noise at work.

The noise assessor provides data on the noise exposure of each employee subject to potentially harmful noise. The noise assessor may recommend that certain workers be enrolled in the employer's hearing surveillance programme.

8.2   How is health surveillance managed?

The employer must ensure that, for each worker who undergoes health surveillance, individual health records are made and kept up-to-date. These records shall contain a summary of the results of the health surveillance relating to fitness-for-work. The records shall be kept in a suitable form that permits further consultation at a later date, taking into account any issues of privacy and data confidentiality.

Copies of the appropriate records shall be supplied, on request, to the appropriate UK government department or agency. Individual worker may have access to their own personal health records.

8.3   What to do if hearing injury is identified

Hearing surveillance may reveal that a worker has an identifiable hearing injury or dysfunction. If in the judgement of a doctor or occupational health-care professional, such an adverse health effect is the result of exposure to noise at work, then certain duties fall upon the employer.

8.3.1   Information for the worker

The worker must be informed, by the doctor or other suitably qualified person, of the results of his or her own personal health surveillance. The worker may request that these health records be made available to some other person of his or her own choice.

8.3.2   Employer actions

Where health surveillance is carried out by a third party, the employer will need to be informed of any significant findings from the health surveillance as they relate to a seafarer's fitness for work involving noise exposure.

Reports on an individual employee should contain only information on fitness to continue with work, unless that individual worker consents to the release of his or her medical information. The employers should also expect to be informed of any significant health surveillance findings in an anonymous form (e.g. for groups of employees).

Any adverse findings place duties upon the employer.

- The employer shall review the risk assessment concerned.

- The employer shall review the noise control measures and hearing protection provision, taking account of advice given by a doctor or occupational heath-care professional, or the Maritime and Coastguard Agency.

- The employer shall consider assigning the affected employee(s) to alternative quieter work, if such is the medical advice.

- Health surveillance should be continued, with special attention given to the hearing health of other seafarers subject to similar noise exposure.

It is worth noting here that the employer must pay the costs of health surveillance carried out in order to comply with the 2007 Noise Regulations.

9 Responsibility – Persons on whom duties are imposed

The 2007 Noise Regulations sets out responsibilities and duties that may apply to the ship owner, down through the hierarchy to individual seafarers.

9.1   Employer's duties

The previous sections of this Code of Practice have enumerated a number of duties that fall upon the employer. There is, however, one aspect that has not been covered. A duty may be imposed upon a person (ship owner, employer etc.). However, if that person has no control over the matter generating that duty, because that person does not have responsibility for the operation of the ship, that duty also extends to any other person who does have effective control of that matter.

9.2   Workers' duties

Workers have duties under the 2007 Noise Regulations.

Workers must make full and proper use of personal hearing protectors and noise control equipment provided by the employer in order to comply with the Regulations.

- Workers should act in accordance with all information, instructions and training provided by the employer in order to comply with the Regulations.

- Workers have a duty to co-operate with the health surveillance programme organised by the employer.

- Prohibition of a levy on any worker

The employer may be required, under the 2007 Noise Regulations, to provide noise control equipment, personal protective equipment or health surveillance services. The employer may not charge, or allow anyone else to charge, any worker for anything done or provided to satisfy the requirements of the regulations.

10 Definitions

These entries are intended for technically-trained readers, but not necessarily noise specialists. A degree of mathematical knowledge is assumed.

Throughout these definitions, the Merchant Shipping and Fishing Vessels (Control of Noise at Work) Regulations 2007 will be referred to as the 2007 Noise Regulations.

Certain definitions from these regulations are given immediately below.

Civil protection services

Include the fire and rescue services, ambulance services, and search-and-rescue services provided by any other person or organisation

Employer

A person or corporate body by whom a worker is employed on a ship under a contract of employment.

Public service activities

Include the activities of HM Coastguard, HM Revenue and Customs, the armed forces, immigration officers, police, prison officers, and the security and intelligence services

Worker

Any person employed on a ship under a contract of employment, including a trainee or apprentice other than any person who is training in a commercial yacht or sail training vessel. Throughout this Code of Practice, the words *employee*, *seafarer* and *crew member* are also used to mean *worker*.

The remainder of the definitions deal with acoustic concepts, and are arranged alphabetically.

Absorption coefficient

The proportion of incident sound energy that is absorbed by a surface or a material.

Action Values and Limit Values

The 2007 Noise Regulations list Lower and Upper Exposure Action Values and Exposure Limit Values. These values are given as Daily Personal Noise Exposure $L_{EP,d}$ or Weekly Personal Noise Exposure $L_{EP,w}$; these exposures are measured in A-weighted Sound Level L_{Aeq}. There is also a C-weighted instantaneous peak sound pressure level L_{Cpeak}. If these levels are reached, various actions are to be taken by employer and employee.

The Lower Exposure Action Values are:

80 dB(A) $L_{EP,d}$ or 80 dB(A) $L_{EP,w}$ i.e. a personal noise exposure of 80 dB(A measured on a daily or weekly basis, or

135 dB(C) L_{Cpeak} i.e. a peak sound pressure level of 135 dB(C).

The Upper Exposure Action Values are:

85 dB(A) $L_{EP,d}$ or 85 dB(A) $L_{EP,w}$, or

137 dB(C) L_{Cpeak}.

The Exposure Limit Values are:

87 dB(A) $L_{EP,d}$ or 87 dB(A) $L_{EP,w}$, or

140 dB(C) L_{Cpeak}.

Neither limit value may be exceeded.

Ambient noise

The background noise or prevailing general noise in an area or compartment.

Assumed protection

Of a personal hearing protector, at a specified frequency. In British practice, the mean attenuation minus the standard deviation for a typical group of wearers, as determined by a standard procedure. In reality, an optimistic estimate of protection.

Attenuation

Reduction of transmitted sound level, used in sound insulation and hearing protection.

Audiogram

A chart or table of a person's hearing threshold levels for pure tones of different frequencies.

Audiometer

A pure-tone audiometer is an electro-acoustical instrument, usually equipped (for air conduction) with two earphones on a headband. The instrument provides pure tones of known frequencies and adjustable magnitude, used to determine hearing threshold levels, one ear at a time. For bone conduction, the audiometer is also equipped with a bone vibrator. In the industrial context, only the air conduction facility is normally required or provided. A *manual* audiometer is one in which the signal presentations, frequency and hearing level selection, and the noting of the subject's responses are performed manually. A *self-recording* audiometer (also known as an *automatic-recording* audiometer) is one in which the signal presentations, hearing level variation, frequency selection or variation, and the recording of the subject's responses are done automatically.

Audiometry

Measurement of a person's hearing threshold levels for pure tones by air conduction under monaural earphone listening conditions, or by bone conduction.

Auricle

The ear flap protruding on each side of the head; sometimes called the pinna.

A-weighted sound level

The sound pressure level of a signal which has been passed through an 'A' filter whereby both low- and high-frequency components are attenuated without affecting the components near 1000 Hz. The unit is the decibel but it is usual to distinguish between this and other uses of the decibel by writing the unit as dB(A). See *frequency weighting*.

Bandwidth

A frequency interval which has an upper and lower limit, and includes all the frequencies within this range.

Calibrator

A highly stable electroacoustic device producing a signal of known frequency at a known sound pressure level; used to calibrate a *sound level meter.* A calibration check is performed in the field, before and after a field test, using a reference sound signal of known frequency and sound pressure level. Such a field check is different from a reference calibration. This is an extensive test to verify the correct functioning of the meter functions; a reference calibration may be performed by the instrument-maker, or by a certified testing organisation. The reference calibration must be traceable back to the National Physical Laboratory.

Cochlea

he spiral-shaped organ of the inner ear containing hair cells, which respond to pressure fluctuations and generate nerve impulses interpreted by the brain as sound.

Competent person

A person with the appropriate combination of skill, knowledge, qualifications and experience needed to perform a satisfactory risk assessment or noise assessment.

C-weighted sound level

The sound pressure level of a signal which has been passed through a 'C' filter that allows passage of frequencies between 20 Hz and 20 kHz. This range is widely recognised as the frequency range of human hearing. The unit is the decibel but it is usual to distinguish between this and other uses of the decibel by writing the unit as dB(C). See also *frequency weighting.*

Damping

The removal of energy from a vibrating system by frictional or viscous forces; the energy removed is converted into heat.

Decibel (dB)

The unit for measuring the relative magnitude of a quantity, based on a logarithmic scale. See also *sound pressure level* and *A-weighted sound level*.

Deafness

A term sometimes used loosely to indicate *hearing loss*. The word *deafness* should be avoided, as it can also mean total extinction of the sensation of hearing.

Diffraction

Change of direction of travel of a sound wave by complex interaction of wavefronts.

Direct field

That part of the acoustic field in a reflecting enclosure where sound coming directly from the source is dominant. Contrast with *reverberant field*.

Earmuff

A hearing protector comprising two ear-cups, each covering the pinna or auricle and having a soft ring to be pressed against the head, to form a noise-tight seal around the auricle.

Earplug

A hearing protector which is inserted into the ear canal.

Ear defender

See *hearing protector*.

Ear protector

See *hearing protector*.

Equivalent continuous sound pressure level

The notional steady sound pressure level, which would cause the same sound energy to be received as that due to the actual (fluctuating) sound over the total duration. The symbol is L_{eq}. When the sound pressure is A-weighted, the symbol should be written L_{Aeq}.

Far field

That part of a free acoustic field distant from the sound source, where energy is radiated as sound. Contrast with *near field.*

Filter

An electronic circuit that modifies the frequency spectrum of a signal while it is in electrical form, within a sound-measuring instrument.

Frequency

The rate of pressure fluctuations that constitute a sound. The unit is the hertz (Hz), equal to one cycle per second. High frequencies can conveniently be expressed in kilohertz (kHz), indicating thousands of hertz.

Frequency weighting

Modification of the frequency spectrum of a signal by means of a filter having a standardised characteristic. The A and C weightings are the most commonly used. The Z weighting is a linear frequency response passing (without any alteration) all components within a very wide range, for instance 2 Hz to 50 kHz.

Hearing loss

The amount, expressed in decibels, by which an individual's hearing threshold level has changed for the worse, as a result of some adverse influence.

Hearing protector

A general term embracing earmuff, earplug and helmet (or other noise-excluding device) worn on the head, to protect the hearing from damage by loud sound.

Hearing threshold level

A measured threshold of hearing, expressed in decibels relative to audiometric zero, the threshold of hearing for young persons with healthy ears.

Hertz (Hz)

The unit of frequency. See *frequency.*

Impact/impulse noise

A noise event of short duration that occurs as an isolated event, or as one of a series of events with a repetition rate of less than 15 per second. The term *impulse* noise usually implies sudden release of new gas into the atmosphere, as would happen with a gunshot. In contrast, *impact* noise results from a collision between two masses, such as a hammer blow on metal.

Infrasound

Sound of frequency less than 20 Hz, i.e. below the normal frequency range of human hearing and thus inaudible. Contrast with *ultrasound.*

Intensity

Widely but incorrectly used for any quantity relating to the amount of sound, such as the amplitude, pressure or power of the sound. For acousticians, sound intensity is the sound power transmitted through an area of 1 square metre, when that unit area is perpendicular to the direction of energy flow in a sound field.

Loudness

An observer's auditory impression of the strength of a sound.

Near field

That part of an acoustic field within a few wavelengths of a sound source, from which some the energy of fluid motion is not radiated away as sound. Contrast with *far field.*

Noise

In the context of assessing hearing hazard, any audible sound should be regarded as noise. *Wide-band* noise consists of a wide range of frequencies. *Random noise* is a signal whose instantaneous value varies randomly with time.

Noise-induced hearing loss (NIHL)

A hearing loss partially or entirely attributable to exposure to high-level noise for a long time. The NIHL is the result of damage to nerve cells in the cochlea (the inner ear).

Octave

An interval on the frequency scale: there is a frequency ratio of 2 to 1 between the highest and lowest frequencies of the interval. An *octave band* has a bandwidth one octave wide, centred at standardised values eg 1 kHz, 2 kHz, 4 kHz and so on. The sound pressure level of a sound which has been passed through an octave band-pass filter is termed the *octave band sound pressure level.* Similarly for *one-third octave bands,* there being three such bands in each octave band.

Peak sound pressure

The greatest instantaneous sound pressure during a stated time interval, regardless of sign (positive or negative pressure excursion).

Permanent threshold shift

The component of hearing threshold shift which shows no progressive recovery with the passage of time when the apparent cause has been removed. *Noise-induced threshold shift* is associated with a noise exposure. *Age-related threshold shift* is related to natural ageing. It is usually assumed that these components are additive, at least for small values of threshold shift due to age and noise.

Pitch

That attribute of auditory sensation related primarily to frequency.

Presbyacusis

Hearing loss which accompanies ageing; mainly affecting high-frequency hearing.

Pure tone

A sound having a single frequency whose sound pressure varies sinusoidally with time.

"Real world" attenuation

The realistic performance of a hearing protector, taking account of poor fitting (especially with ear plugs), long hair and the wearing of spectacles (especially with ear muffs), all of which can reduce the ideal performance of hearing protectors, as published by the manufacturer.

Reference pressure

20 μPa (micropascals), used in the definition of sound pressure levels and frequency-weighted sound levels.

Reverberant field

That part of an acoustic field within a reflecting enclosure where reflected sound (echo) is dominant. Contrast with *direct field.*

Risk assessment

Consideration of the level, type and duration of exposure to a noise hazard (including any exposure to impact/impulse noise), and any effects on the health and safety of workers at particular risk from such an exposure. Can also apply to other hazards, such as electricity or chemicals.

Sound

Mechanical disturbance propagated in air (an elastic medium), of such character as to be capable of exciting the sensation of hearing.

Sound level meter (SLM); integrating-averaging SLM

An instrument designed to measure a frequency-weighted value of the sound pressure level. Modern SLMs typically have an "averaging" mode; the instrument provides a direct reading, over a noise sample duration, of the equivalent continuous sound pressure level L_{eq}, or L_{Aeq} if the A-weighting is selected. If the SLM has an "integrating" mode, it reads *Sound Exposure Level* L_{EA} directly. With suitable circuitry, the SLM can also perform frequency analyses, usually in either octave or one-third octave bands.

Sound pressure

At a point in a medium, the difference between the pressure existing at the instant considered and the static or atmospheric pressure. Sound pressure is measured in *pascals* (Pa); 1 Pa $= 1$ newton per square metre (N/m^2). Sometimes called acoustic pressure.

Sound pressure level (SPL)

The sound pressure level of a sound, in decibels, is equal to 20 times the logarithm (to the base 10) of the ratio of the sound pressure to the reference pressure 20 μPa (for the avoidance of doubt, 20×10^{-6} Pa).

Temporary threshold shift

The component of threshold shift which shows progressive recovery with the passage of time when the apparent cause has been removed.

Threshold of hearing

The minimum level of a sound which is just audible in given conditions, for a specified fraction of presentations (conventionally 50%).

Threshold shift

The difference, in decibels, of the hearing threshold levels of a person, measured on two separate occasions. If the threshold shift progressively improves with the passage of time when the cause (usually noise) has ceased; it is referred to as *temporary threshold shift*. If there is no improvement with time, it is *permanent threshold shift* (PTS).

Tinnitus

A subjective sense of 'noise in the head' or 'ringing in the ears' that is not directly due to any real sound. It can be associated with exposure to high levels of noise; noise-induced tinnitus can be temporary or permanent. Tinnitus can also arise through natural causes.

Transmission loss

The attenuation or reduction of sound pressure level across a wall or barrier.

Ultrasound

Sound of frequency greater than 20 kHz, i.e. above the normal frequency range of human hearing and thus inaudible. Contrast with *infrasound*.

Wavelength

The distance between successive wave-fronts of a sinusoidal wave propagating in a medium. A long wavelength corresponds to a low frequency.

Regulation Number	Person responsible	When	Requirement
9	employer	lower action value exceeded	provide suitable and sufficient information, instruction, training to workers and representatives.
10.1	employer	identified hearing risk	health surveillance for workers.
10.2	employer	lower action value exceeded	preventative (informative or monitoring) hearing tests for workers.
10.2	employer	upper action value exceeded	hearing examined/assessed by doctor.
10.3	doctor	employee hearing deficit	assess: noise damage to hearing? doctor may wish to refer employee for specialist examination.
10.4	employer	noise damage to hearing	• inform employee; • review risk assessment, personal hearing protection, control measures; • consider alternative work for employee.
11	employer	documented hearing risk	consult with workers or representatives: • risk assessment; • measures to reduce risk; • health surveillance; • choice of personal hearing protectors.
12	workers	documented hearing risk	• make full and proper use of hearing protectors and noise control equipment (and health surveillance); • follow instructions/training provided.

Appendix B
Extracts from relevant Notices and Regulations

From Marine Guidance Note 352:

Daily Exposure to Different Sound Levels: Annex 1

Recommended maximum limits for different areas onboard ship.

The limits below should be regarded as maximum levels, rather than desirable levels, and as appropriate take account of the attenuation (noise reduction) that can be achieved with ear protectors.

Area	Recommended Limit dB(A)
Machinery spaces – general	90
Machinery spaces – unmanned	110
Machinery control rooms	75
Wheelhouse/bridge/chart room/radar room	65
Bridge wings	70
Radio room/communications centre	60
Galleys, serveries, pantries	75
Normally unoccupied spaces	90
Sleeping cabins, day cabins, hospital	60
Offices, conferences rooms, etc.	65
Mess rooms, recreation rooms, recreation areas	65
Open deck areas	75
Corridors, changing rooms, bathrooms, lockers and similar spaces	80
Ship's whistle	110

Appendix C

Method of calculating Personal Noise Exposure using the HSE Ready Reckoner: Worked examples for daily and weekly exposures

Consider a hypothetical "noise day" for an engine-room attendant, as seen in the figure below. The horizontal axis is hours spent in the engine room; the vertical axis is L_{Aeq} sampled during several tasks.

The $L_{EP,d}$ cannot be estimated from the figure, except to say that it will be high, indeed very high. If the "noise day" is expressed in words, as below, then calculation of $L_{EP,d}$ is easier to manage. The components of the "noise day" may be evaluated in Exposure Points found in the HSE Ready Reckoner, Table C1 at the end of this Appendix.

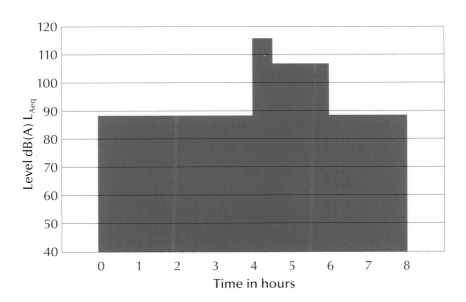

task	observed dB(A) L_{Aeq}	task duration, hours
general engine room duties, away from engines.	87	4
bleed high-pressure-air storage bottles.	114	0.5
planned maintenance of one of a pair of diesel engines, adjacent engine essential running.	105	1.5
general engine room duties, away from engines.	87	2

C.1   Calculation of $L_{EP,d}$

Consider the first part of the day: 87 dB(A) for 4 hours. Find the Ready Reckoner row for 87 dB(A); find the column for 4 hours. Find the intersection of the column and row. This noise exposure is worth 80 Exposure Points.

Now proceed to the next noise period. This is a challenge: 114 dB(A) for 0.5 hour. There is no row for 114 dB(A). But remember that you can trade off level against duration: a doubling of duration brings a reduction of 3 dB so that:

114 dB(A) for 0.5 hour

contains the same acoustic energy as

111 dB(A) for 1 hour

which itself contains the same acoustic energy as

108 dB(A) for 2 hours

This "noise day" component, 114 dB(A) for 0.5 hour, is worth 5 000 Exposure Points.

Now for the third component 105 dB(A) for 1.5 hours. Break it up into convenient times, as:

105 dB(A) for 1 hour equals   1300 points

105 dB(A) for 0.5 hour equals   630 points

Total equals   1900 Exposure Points

The last component is simple: 87 dB(A) for 2 hours is worth 40 Exposure Points.

The sum of all the work tasks/periods is 7020 Exposure Points. Go to the extreme-right two columns of the Ready Reckoner: Total Exposure Points and $L_{EP,d}$. The total of 7020 points indicates an $L_{EP,d}$ about midway between 103 dB(A) and 104 dB(A) $L_{EP,d}$. The nearest half a decibel is quite satisfactory: 103.5 dB(A) $L_{EP,d}$.

Please go to Table C2 at the end of this Appendix, to see how this noise day might be represented on the worksheet mentioned in section 6.6.4.2 Measurement procedure.

C.2   Calculation of $L_{EP,w}$

Having the Exposure Points for one "noise day", it is relatively easy to arrive at the exposure for a "noise week", that is for a notional five-day working week. Imagine a week during which the example engine-room attendant spends three days in the noise already quantified as 7020 Exposure Points. The rest of the week is spent on quiet tasks, perhaps task scheduling or planned maintenance. The total exposure would be:

workday	Exposure Points
day 1	7020
day 2	7020
day 3	7020
days 4 and 5	0
TOTAL over week	21060

The Exposure Point total is divided by 5, to give 4212 points. Go back to the two right-hand columns of Table C1 at the end of this Appendix. The weekly average of 4212 points is between 91 dB(A) and 92 dB(A); call it 91.5 dB(A) rounded up to the nearest half-decibel. The answer is 91.5 dB(A) $L_{EP,w}$, with the acoustic energy of the three "noise days" **spread out** over a notional five-day week. This weekly noise exposure is greater than the Upper Exposure Action Value of the 2007 Noise Regulations.

Consider a different scenario. If the example engine-room attendant spent seven consecutive days in the noise already quantified as 7020 Exposure Points per day, then the total number of points would be:

7 days X 7020 Exposure Points per day = 49140 Exposure Points over the week

The total for the week must now be **compressed** into a notional five-day week: divide the total by five to get 9828 points. Again, go back to the two right-hand columns of the Table C1. The weekly average of 9828 points is very close to 10 000 points, making a weekly exposure of 105 dB(A) $L_{EP,w}$. Again, this weekly noise exposure is greater than the second action value of the 2007 Noise Regulations.

Table C1 Exposure Points for various levels and durations

L_{eq} dB(A)	Exposure Points for durations (full or partial)								total	
	¼ hour	½ hour	1 hour	2 hours	4 hours	8 hours	10 hours	12 hours	EP	$L_{EP,d}$
110	1,000	2,000	4,000	8,000	16,000				32,000	110
109	800	1,600	3,200	6,300	13,000				25,000	109
108	630	1,300	2,500	5,000	10,000				20,000	108
107	500	1,000	2,000	4,000	8,000	16,000			16,000	107
106	400	800	1,600	3,200	6,300	13,000	16,000		13,000	106
105	320	630	1,300	2,500	5,000	10,000	13,000	16,000	10,000	105
104	250	500	1,000	2,000	4,000	8,000	10,000	13,000	8,000	104
103	200	400	800	1,600	3,200	6,300	8,000	10,000	6,300	103
102	160	320	630	1,300	2,500	5,000	6,300	8,000	5,000	102
101	130	250	500	1,000	2,000	4,000	5,000	6,300	4,000	101
100	100	200	400	800	1,600	3,200	4,000	5,000	3,200	100
99	80	160	320	630	1,300	2,500	3,200	4,000	2,500	99
98	63	130	250	500	1,000	2,000	2,500	3,200	2,000	98
97	50	100	200	400	800	1,600	2,000	2,500	1,600	97
96	40	80	160	320	630	1,300	1,600	2,000	1,300	96
95	32	63	130	250	500	1,000	1,300	1,600	1,000	95
94	25	50	100	200	400	800	1,000	1,300	800	94
93	20	40	80	160	320	630	800	1,000	630	93
92	16	32	63	130	250	500	630	800	500	92
91	13	25	50	100	200	400	500	630	400	91
90	10	20	40	80	160	320	400	500	320	90
89	8	16	32	63	130	250	320	400	250	89
88	6	13	25	50	100	200	250	320	200	88
87	5	10	20	40	80	160	200	250	160	87
86	4	8	16	32	63	130	160	200	130	86
85	3	6	13	25	50	100	130	160	100	85
84		5	10	20	40	80	100	130	80	84
83		4	8	16	32	63	80	100	63	83
82		3	6	13	25	50	63	80	50	82
81			5	10	20	40	50	63	40	81

Table C2 Measurement observations and results

name/job	activity/location/tool use	position on ship plan*	time of day*	sample duration	meas. level, LAeq	exposure duration	Exposure Points	LEP,d	LCpeak	see remarks below
	general engine room duties			3 min	87	4 hr	80			(1)
A. Name, engine room attendant	bleed air bottles			10 min	114	0.5 hr	5,000		139	(2) (3)
	diesel maintenance			8 min	105	1.5 hr				
	general engine room duties			3 min	87					(1)
	COMPLETE DAY									(4)

* not necessary for this example

Numbered remarks (from above):

(1) away from engines, in sound refuge with control and gauges for engines: these two periods in sound refuge > upper exposure action value; ensure/enforce use of hearing protection in refuge; long term – recommend new sound refuge with higher transmission loss (attenuation)

(2) air bottles exhaust directly into engine room: recommend exhaust silencer, or recommend exhaust vented to outside air

(3) bleeding air bottles: L_{Cpeak} at worker's ear > upper exposure action value

(4) this $L_{EP,d}$ >> upper exposure action value: confirm that worker's ear muffs provide sufficient protection

Appendix D

Format for reporting results of a ship noise survey

Whilst the 2007 Noise Regulations do not specify the format for any noise survey report, a report in the form set out below will properly record the survey results and recommendations. This report should be retained by the employer; in addition, it might usefully be carried onboard the vessel to which it applies.

OCCUPATIONAL HEALTH AND SAFETY INSPECTION
HAND-TRANSMITTED VIBRATION ASSESSMENT
UNITED KINGDOM REGISTERED VESSELS

Name of vessel		Type of vessel	
Company or owner		Port of registry	
Official number		IMO number	

Main Engine		Main Engine Type	
Power Output		Number of Engines	
Number of Cylinders (and bore)		Running Speed (RPM)	

Propulsion System		Number of Shafts or Outputs	

Generator Engine		Generator Engine Type	
Generator Engine Output		Number of Generators	

Number of Cylinders (and bore)		Running Speed (RPM)	

Sound Level Meter: Manufacturer, Model		Serial Number	
Class of Meter		Meter Certificate Number	
Calibrator: Manufacturer, Model		Serial Number	
Class of Calibrator		Calibrator Certificate Number	
Calibration Tone Frequency		Calibration Tone Level	
Date of Noise Measurements		Start Time and Finish Time	
Starting Calibration Tone Level		Finishing Calibration Tone Level	

Noise assessor		Official Stamp
Assessor's signature		
Assessor's office address		
Date of report		

General Notes/Comments

create more space as needed

List any spaces non-compliant with the 2007 Noise Regulations (required)

Category of space	Measurement location on attached plan or sketch	lower exposure action value exceeded for any worker: Yes/No, $L_{EP,d}$ or L_{Cpeak}?	upper exposure action value exceeded for any worker: Yes/No, $L_{EP,d}$ or L_{Cpeak}?
	create more rows as needed		

Summary of measurements

This section is intended to summarise the measurements from individual compartments, spaces or areas (given in full in the noise reading sheets for individual workers). Record the maximum Sound Level measured in each category of space.

Category of space	Measurement location on attached plan or sketch	maximum value of L_{Aeq}	maximum value of L_{Ceq}	maximum value of L_{Cpeak}
	create more rows as needed			

List the noise abatement measures (required by the 2007 Noise Regulations)

Category of space	Measurement location(s) where measures apply (see attached plan or sketch)	Technical measures	Organisational measures
create more rows as needed			

Recommended noise abatement measures
(indicate location on attached plan or sketch)

create more space as needed

E.3   Using the attenuation information

E3.1 The SNR value

The SNR (single number rating) method is the simplest way to *approximate* what $L_{A\,protected}$ would be heard "underneath" a hearing protector. For a quick decision on hearing protector, the HSE guidance is:

for a noise level L_A	select a protector with an SNR value of
85-90 dB(A)	20 or less
90-95	20-30
95-100	25-35
100-105	30 or more

To amplify this advice, a simple equation is given in the HSE (2005) guidance document:

$$L'_A = L_C - SNR$$

Note: the symbol L'_A (L^{prime}_A) is used to avoid any potential confusion with the L_A measured for the noise in question. For any real noise, the only measurement needed is L_C from the noise survey. The SNR value is given by the hearing protector manufacturer. The subtraction is straightforward.

In real use, however, the attenuation of any hearing protector can be less than predicted by manufacturer's data. To give a realistic estimate, by allowing for the imperfect fitting and condition of hearing protectors in the working environment, the Health and Safety Executive recommends that a "real-world" factor of 4 dB be applied to make the plug or muff *less* protective, as given below:

$$L_{A\,protected} = L_C - SNR + 4\ dB$$

It is worth noting that the SNR method is based solely on an overall sound pressure level, without regard to spectral content.

E3.2   The HML values

These values are a high-frequency attenuation value H, a medium-frequency attenuation value M, and a low-frequency attenuation value L. These values are used to calculate a Predicted Noise Reduction (PNR) based upon the L_A and L_C measurements for the offending noise.

For noises with measured levels such that $(L_C - L_A) \leq 2$ dB (not much low-frequency energy):

$$PNR = M - \left\{ \frac{H - M}{4} \; (L_C - L_A - 2 \text{ dB}) \right\}$$

Otherwise, $(L_C - L_A) > 2$ dB (for noises with considerable low-frequency energy)

$$PNR = M - \left\{ \frac{M - L}{8} \; (L_C - L_A - 2 \text{ dB}) \right\}$$

The PNR should be subtracted from the L_A reading observed for the offending noise, to give the notional protected level.

$$L'_A = L_A - PNR$$

Again, to account for the "real world" factors, 4 dB is added to give a realistic estimate of the protected level heard underneath the Personal Hearing Protectors:

$$L_{A \text{ protected}} = L_A - PNR + 4 \text{ dB}$$

Note that the HML method uses the A-weighted sound level of the offending noise. The L_A takes account of the spectrum of the actual noise.

E.3.3   The octave-band method

It may be argued that the octave-band method gives the most accurate calculation of the protection provided by PHP. Also, it is considerable more involved than the SNR and HML methods.

There are two problems for anybody trying to assess the suitability of PHP using the octave-band method. Firstly, the octave-band calculations will require values for the A-weighting frequency response. The values below come from BS EN 61672-1, the British Standard on sound level meters.

octave-band centre freq., Hz	A-weighting response, dB
16	−56.7
31.5	−39.4
63	−26.2
125	−16.1
250	−8.6
500	−3.2
1,000	0
2,000	1.2
4,000	1
8,000	−1.1
16,000	−6.6

Secondly, the octave-band method requires a degree of proficiency with decibel addition. Please refer to Table E1 given on the next page. This Table give a matrix of arbitrary level points that may be assigned to any decibel value of interest. The left-hand column give decibels in intervals of ten. The top row gives decibels in unit intervals. An example should make clear the use of the Table.

What would be the decibel value if two noise sources are heard simultaneously: 87 dB and 92 dB?

What level-point-value would be assigned to 87 dB? Find the row marked 80 dB, find the column marked 7 dB. The intersection of the row and column indicates 160 level-points.

Repeat the process for 92 dB. The intersection of the appropriate row and column indicates 500 level-points.

The two simultaneous noises would be represented as the sum of the individual level-points: 160 points + 500 points = 660 points. Search the table for this value or one very close to it: 630 level-points represents 93 dB. Therefore

87 dB + 92 dB = 93 dB

Table E1. Arbitrary level points for decibel addition

dB	0	1	2	3	4	5	6	7	8	9
60	0.3	0.4	0.5	0.6	0.8	1	1.3	1.6	2	2.5
70	3.2	4	5	6.3	8	10	13	16	20	25
80	32	40	50	63	80	100	130	160	200	250
90	320	400	500	630	800	1,000	1,300	1,600	2,000	2,500
100	3,200	4,000	5,000	6,300	8,000	10,000	13,000	16,000	20,000	25,000

An easy explanatory example to aid the reader's understanding of how the arbitrary level points are used for decibel addition:

91 dB + 91 dB ≠ 182 dB

91 dB has been assigned 400 arbitrary level points

2 X 400 points = 800 points

800 points indicates that 91 dB + 91 dB = 94 dB

Always keep this in mind: X dB plus X dB equals X+3 dB

Now for an example that may require estimating decimal points of a decibel:

90 dB + 80 dB = ??

90 dB has been assigned 320 arbitrary level points.

80 dB has been assigned 32 arbitrary level points.

320 points + 32 points = 352 points

350 points falls near to the midpoint between 320 and 400; the answer is very close to 90.5 dB.

Any answer to the nearest 0.5 dB is quite satisfactory in practical acoustics.

Returning to the octave-band method of assessing the protection offer by PHP, the method will require an octave band analysis of the offending noise, reduced by the PHP manufacturer's attenuation data, further reduced by the A-weighting response, to result in the A-weighted octave-band levels heard in the ear. These bands-in-the-ear are then transformed to level-points for addition. The level-point-total is then transformed back into a protected dB(A) value. In words, this process may seem difficult to follow; a worked example (provided later) should make the process clear.

E.3.4 Worked examples

In order to examine how the attenuation information may be used, it is first necessary to have a loud noise to work on. Look at the octave-band spectrum of Figure E1 below. The horizontal axis is octave-band centre frequency, from 16 Hz to 16 000 Hz (16 kHz). The vertical axis is band level averaged over a suitable sample duration, in dB $L_{eq,band}$ (note that the band levels are not subject to a frequency weighting). This particular noise is very loud, with strong low-frequency components. The low-frequency emphasis is plain from the observed levels:

$$L_{Aeq} = 104.5 \text{ dB(A)}$$

$$L_{Ceq} = 120 \text{ dB(C)}$$

The A-weighting network discriminates strongly against low-frequency components; the C-weighting passes most of the low-frequency acoustic energy.

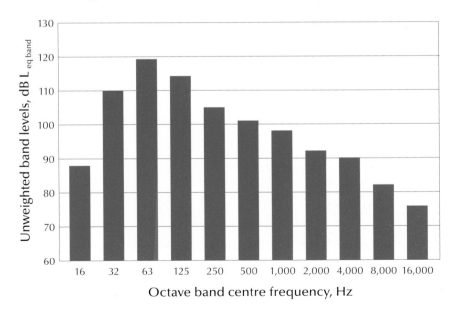

Figure E1 The octave band spectrum of a noise to be used in worked examples for the three methods of assessing protection offered by PHP.

These two quantities should be measured for any occupational noise onboard a ship being surveyed. It is possible to assess the suitability of hearing protectors using these values.

The octave-band levels will be used later to calculate the $L_{A\,protected}$ "underneath" a hearing protector. But first, the discussion will deal with estimating the $L_{A\,protected}$ from simpler measurements of the noise.

E.3.4.1   Using the SNR method to assess an ear plug

Given below are the manufacturer's attenuation data for a cylindrical plastic foam ear plug.

Plastic foam ear plug, cylindrical shape

frequency, Hz	63	125	250	500	1,000	2,000	4,000	8,000
mean atten, dB	22.3	23.3	24.6	26.9	27.4	34.1	41.6	40.4
std dev, dB	5.4	5.3	3.6	5.4	4.8	3.1	3.5	6.4
assumed protection	16.9	18.0	21.0	21.5	22.6	31.0	38.1	34.0
	SNR	28	H	30	M	24	L	22

The SNR calculation is simple: $L'_A = L_C - SNR$. Including the 4 dB "real world" adjustment gives:

$$L_{A\,protected} = L_C - SNR + 4\ dB$$

Filling in the values for L_C and SNR gives:

$$L_{A\,protected} = 120\ dB\ L_C - 28\ dB\ SNR + 4\ dB = 96\ dB(A)$$

This protected level 96 dB(A) is very high: any (protected) exposure duration longer than 30-40 minutes would result in a breach of the exposure limit value 87 dB(A) $L_{EP,d}$. This ear plug does not provide sufficient protection, according to the SNR estimation.

E.3.4.2 Using the HML method to assess a set of ear muffs

Here are the manufacturer's attenuation data for a set of heavy-duty, high-attenuation ear muffs.

frequency, Hz	63	125	250	500	1,000	2,000	4,000	8,000
mean atten, dB	21.8	16.9	24.3	34.5	40.3	39.5	41.7	41.2
std dev, dB	4.0	2.5	2.9	2.3	2.0	2.6	2.0	2.1
assumed protection	17.8	14.4	21.4	32.2	38.3	36.9	39.7	39.1
	SNR	34	H	39	M	31	L	22

For the noise of Figure E1, the observed levels were

$$L_{Ceq} = 120 \ dB(C)$$

$$L_{Aeq} = 104.5 \ dB(A)$$

$$L_{Ceq} - L_{Aeq} = 15.5 \ dB \gg 2 \ dB$$

For noises with considerable low-frequency energy, this form of the Predicted Noise Reduction equation is used:

$$PNR = M - \left\{ \frac{M - L}{8} \ (L_C - L_A - 2 \ dB) \right\}$$

Filling in the manufacturer's HML values gives:

$$PNR = 31 - \left\{ \frac{31 - 22}{8} \ (15.5 \ dB - 2 \ dB) \right\}$$

$$PNR = 15.8 \ dB$$

The PNR should be subtracted from the L_A reading observed for the offending noise, to give the notional protected level:

$$L'_A = L_A - PNR$$

Again, to account for the "real world" factors, 4 dB is added to give a realistic estimate of the protected level heard underneath the Personal Hearing Protectors:

$$L_{A \ protected} = L_A - PNR + 4 \ dB = 104.5 \ dB(A) - 15.8 \ dB + 4 \ dB$$

$$= 93.7 \ dB \approx 93.5 \ dB$$

This protected level 93.5 dB(A) is very high: any (protected) exposure duration longer than about 1 hour would result in a breach of the exposure limit value 87 dB(A) $L_{EP,d}$. This model of ear muffs does not provide sufficient protection, according to the HML estimation.

E.3.4.3 Using the octave-band method to assess ear plugs used under ear muffs, as dual protection

For very high noise levels, it may be necessary to use plugs under muffs. Here is the manufacturer's attenuation data for the cylindrical foam plugs used in combination with the high-attenuation muffs.

frequency, Hz	63	125	250	500	1,000	2,000	4,000	8,000
mean atten, dB	31.2	29.6	34.2	72.2	42.6	41.4	50.8	46.7
std dev, dB	6.6	6.6	7.9	8.3	7.3	3.7	4.3	4.4
assumed protection	24.6	23.1	23.3	33.9	35.3	37.7	46.5	42.3
SNR	38	H	39	M	35	L	29	

The octave-band calculations may be seen in the matrix below. The left-hand column (1) gives the octave band centre frequencies; the next column (2) gives the band sound pressure levels for the indicated centre frequencies. Column 3 gives the A-weighting frequency response, which is subtracted from or added to (as appropriate) the values in (2); the result (4) is A-weighted band level. The Assumed Protection (5) comes from the attenuation data above. Column (4) minus column (5) gives protected A-weighted band levels (6) which are finally transformed into arbitrary level points (7) using the values found above in Table E1.

(column 1)	(2)	(3)	(4)	(5)	(6)	(7)
octave-band centre freq., Hz	band level, dB	A-wt.	A-wt. band level, dB	Assum. Prot. Value, dB	protected A-wt band level, dB	arbitrary level points
16	88	−56.7	31.3	–		
31.5	110	−39.4	70.6	–		
63	119	−26.2	92.8	24.6	68.2	2
125	114	−16.1	97.9	23.1	74.8	9.5
250	105	−8.6	96.4	23.3	73.1	6.3
500	101	−3.2	97.8	33.9	63.9	0.8
1,000	98	0	98	35.3	62.5	0.6
2,000	92	1.2	93.2	37.7	55.5	<0.12
4,000	90	1	91	46.5	44.5	<0.01
8,000	82	−1.1	80.9	42.3	38.6	<0.01
16,000	76	−6.6	69.4	–		
				total arbitrary level points		19.2
			protected L_A (underneath the plug/muff combination)			78.0 dB(A)
			add 4 dB for real-world protected L_A (underneath the plug/muff combination)			82.0 dB(A)

italics = estimated or interpolated value

The total level points transform back to 78.0 dB(A). The 4 dB "real world" penalty is applied, to give the final answer 82 dB(A) $L_{A\ protected}$.

This is a useful result. The protected level is less than the upper exposure action value of the 2007 Noise Regulations. The plugs-plus-muffs combination provides adequate protection against the 104.5 dB(A) L_{Aeq} noise, allowing the wearer to work in that noise for a full eight-hour shift.